CONV
BETWEEN WOMEN
The Stories That Heal Us

MW01172475

Authors

Kathryn Simpson Baskette

Kendra Kautz

Jenn Maroney

Zell McFail

Tammy T. Sapp

Kelly Schwartz Keville

Elizabeth Page Shepley

Shannon Sheridan

Credits

Cover design

Blake

linktr.ee/blakecreates

ISBN: 979-8-9850550-7-8

Dedication

For Mei Mei

Contents

Foreword

The idea for this multi-author book collaboration was literally born in my many conversations with women. As a women's empowerment coach and writing mentor, I am in constant conversation with women, both listening to their stories and sharing mine. It's how we connect, how we nurture and grow our relationships with one another. How we understand ourselves and others more deeply.

Throughout my life I have marveled at the women who surround me, cherishing the sense of community we create each time we courageously tell a part of our story. And the healing! The healing that transpires in the storytelling and the story-receiving is magical.

I wanted to create a collection of healing stories written by brilliant and brave women. A book collaboration validating the authors' personal stories of healing, documenting their individual and collective journeys, and ultimately serving other women who need to hear these stories of experience, strength, and hope.

My main purpose in co-publishing this collection of stories is to provide women with stories that bring them comfort, validation, and perhaps… courage to tell their own stories. It is my hope as women read these shared stories they will reach out and connect with the authors, join their communities, and join the conversation between women. Storytelling supports community and healing among us all.

Kelly Schwartz Keville

The Box
Kathryn Simpson Baskette

S itting in my side-by-side, I glanced at the box wrapped in an old blue towel. I decided to take the towel off and hold it in my lap. I looked up as I was unwrapping it and saw a beautiful deer in the field where I had chosen to park. She didn't see me as I blended in with the camo color on my vehicle and outfit.

As I gazed at her eating walnuts and dew-covered grass, my thoughts floated around the field. So many answers I needed. How can I do this on my own? How could he do this to his family? To me? What else did I not know? How can someone seem to live a double life? How could another woman hurt someone so harshly? I did nothing to her. She saw us every day. How do you look at someone daily and be screwing their husband? Who else in this small town knew and said nothing? Could I take care of land and a home all by myself? Who are my enemies? The questions went on and on until I felt dizzy.

I watched the deer prance away. Before going into the woods, she glanced back at me and disappeared. I smiled and grabbed my notebook. I poured my heart onto paper emptying my soul of its pain. It is only a temporary fix, but better than the alternative. I used my box as a portable desk to write.

A poem came from the depths of my being:

"The Blood of Your Sin"

Today you're covered
With the blood of your sin.
Clothes drenched
And vibrant red.

All the hurt and pain
Trickling down your arms
The tears of your wife and children
Mixed with the blood of your harm.

Blood soaking your chest
From secrets and lies
You told so many
There's no reason why.

Blood drips down soaking
Your middle and legs
From fornication
And the sick life you led.

Blood creeps into your shoes.
You feel the squish in your toes.
Walking away from your family,
Leaving them nothing but clothes.

They still pray
That one day you'll see
Your destructive life
Changed theirs completely.

They pray forgiveness
Soaks into their hearts.
They can love you
Though their lives once fell apart.

They pray God takes over
Your body, heart, and mind.
That one day you'll wake up
And your light will begin to shine.

They struggle sometimes
To keep their own heart clean.
It's hard when others judge them
From their pain unseen.

No matter what
They know it's God that counts.
Everyone else knows nothing
Of what God's plan is about.

I decided to wrap up the box in the old navy towel and put it in the back. "I'll wait a little longer," I thought. Closing my notebook, I looked across the field. A prayer unfolded with tears flowing down my cheeks. I put the key in the ignition and made my way back home.

I parked in the driveway and paused to wipe away tears. Looking in the rearview mirror, I made sure there was no makeup smudged or mascara running down my face. I made my way into the house to check on the kids and chores.

I came in to see my daughter filling up the dishwasher. She looked up and smiled, "Mom, I have the clothes going, made your bed and mine, and took the dogs out." I looked at her expression and could see the love radiating from her eyes. "That's why I have to wait one more day," I thought.

I gave her the biggest hug and said, "Thank you so much. I don't know what I would do without you." She replied, "Mom, it's just a few chores. No big deal. Besides, I was dancing and singing to my music, anyway."

I went downstairs to my son's room and peeked in. "Hey, are you up yet? How's the project coming? Do you need any help before class tomorrow?" He replied, "I'm fine. The project's coming and I don't need anything. I'll be ready for class." "Well, just let me know if you need something," I responded.

"And he's the other reason… one more day. I can make it one more day." My mind reasoned.

I grabbed a cup of coffee and sat on the porch. "OK, your day off. What is the plan? You must push the mess of your life aside and get things going for the kids." I made a mental list of tasks, appointments, and chores. I gulped down my coffee. It was quarter to nine already, crap.

Rounding up everyone, we made our way to the car for counseling. I didn't feel like it helped me much, but I was hoping Adam and Sophie were getting something positive from it. Besides, at least we were doing something. I didn't know how much healing was going to come from a disaster this big.

Sophie sat in the seat beside me on the way to town. "Mom, I don't like this lady. Do I have to keep going? It's not really helping me, anyway." I sighed and responded, "Soph, I don't know what else to do. I am doing the best I can. Do you think you can go one more time? Let's just see how this session goes." Tears began creeping up as I took a deep breath and once more shoved emotions deep inside.

We pulled up to the office and filed in. Of course, I was met by the receptionist who gestured for the kids to take a seat. "Your bill is outstanding. What do you have today? It's $50 a piece today and your bill is already $300." I managed to ask, "Has he paid anything yet? I have $100 on me. Sam agreed to pay half for the kids." The secretary began typing and scrolling then looked up at me and shook her head. "Nothing for a month and only $50 then," she whispered. "OK, will you take $100 today? I will work on getting caught up by the next visit. Looking at me with compassion she answered, "I'm sure we can do that, but I have to ask the counselors first."

We waited for what seemed like hours when the secretary got up from her desk. A few minutes later she came back and motioned me to her desk again. "So, are we still good for today?" I asked nervously. The secretary smiled and replied, "Yes, the counselors agreed to split what you have three ways. I will print out your balance for each of you today and email you. Hopefully, you can pass the balance on for the kids, and it will be paid by the next visit.

Adam and Sophie went to their own counselors as I walked in and sat down for my own appointment. No sooner than my butt hit the cushion, the tears began flowing. Everything I had pushed down projected itself like vomit. The words, feelings, and broken heart came flooding to the surface. All of it except the box.

Ms. Jones listened intently and handed me a wad of tissues. She gave me suggestions to "better my life." The list was overwhelming. I had already gone back to work which seemed impossible with all I had going on. I just reminded myself that I wasn't the only one going through divorce and wouldn't be the last.

Going back to school was one of the suggestions she made. I understood and would give it a try, but I had no idea how I was going to juggle that, help my daughter get back on track after losing her job and her father, guide my son in his last year of school and deal with his anger at his dad, and keep a home going as well. How the hell did this lady think I could go to college??

When Sophie got in the car she said, "I am really done with this lady. She basically blamed our situation on you." I put the car in park and looked at her. "What did you say?" Soph replied, "Yeah, she said shame on your mom." "Hold on, what did you say to her? Nevermind, it doesn't even matter. She shouldn't be shaming me or your father. Y'all wait here and I will be right back."

I marched into the office, emotions of anger steaming out of my nose. I took a deep breath and asked to speak with Sophie's counselor for just a moment. The secretary, seeing the redness on my face and the fire out of my ears, quickly responded, "Yes, she hasn't gone into her next appointment yet. I will let her know your request."

A moment later, I was guided to her office and staring at Miss Jamerson. I gathered myself and stepped in for a little chat.

I marched out of the office and slammed the door behind me. I got into the driver's seat and began to sob. I couldn't push the emotions away this time.

Once we were home the kids got out of the car and I remained seated. Sniffling, I called my mom and explained the whole ordeal between sobs. She consoled me as best she could over the phone. Mom offered to help pay Soph's bill the following day. I could pay her back with the next two paychecks.

I walked in and explained to the kids that I was going for a ride in the woods. I needed to calm down. Sophie came up to me with tears in her eyes, "Mom, I'm sorry. I didn't mean to get you into any trouble. I will be careful about what I share from now on. Especially to counselors and doctors." I sighed and looked in her beautiful large blue-green eyes, "Soph, no. You should be able to express yourself in counseling. That's the whole point. You were right. This counselor isn't the right fit. I just wanted you to be sure before throwing in the towel."

As I walked out the door, Sophie began letting out her pain through dancing and singing in her room. Adam returned to his room downstairs to finish his project. I grabbed the box wrapped in the dilapidated towel and headed for the woods.

This time I chose my favorite spot. It's a 200-year-old fireplace, I estimated. Still standing with only a few rocks fallen over the years. My assumption was the vines and trees that grew strategically around had kept it upright for all these years.

This fireplace was one of the reasons we desired the land. I found it as beautiful as the Eiffel Tower. My mind went to the day that we all cleaned the area up. We picked up limbs and raked leaves. Occasionally stopping, excited that one of us found an artifact. It was a little treasure of blue, amber, or aqua glass from an old bottle. Other times, a piece of clay.

I sighed and began rehashing all the events at our appointment in my head. Second guessing the encounter and wondering again how I am going to do all of this on my own. Another thing to add on the "To-Do" list, I noted. Item 1,042... Search for a counselor for Sophie. This one will be bumped up to number one.

The same questions swam around my head once more. The agony and pain welled up inside again. I put the box on my lap and grabbed my journal and pen.

Time is harsh
It robs you blind.
Much worse is my brain,
The words I can't find.

My heart is dust
And my soul bruised.
I'm not sure
I'll make it through.

Woman to woman,
I would love to ask,
What makes you so evil?
What's in your past?

I can only guess
It must've been hell.
For you to hurt others,
Also, yourself.

I know the lies.
There's no need to ask.
You wouldn't tell the truth
Just keep wearing your mask.

Underneath you are smiling

And holding your knife.
I wonder if you know
It's not just my life.

It's my children
And yours
My family and his
And also, yours.

Keep a grip.
Hold onto it tight.
One day you may slip
And take your own life.

What you think is so great
Is going to end.
People like you
Don't ever win.

I peeked inside the box, and all was still there. Safe inside. I looked up and saw a squirrel grab an acorn and stuff it in his mouth. He began swirling around each rock of the old fireplace. He was celebrating and looking for more deliciousness in his life. I sighed and thought, "One day I'm going to get through this. I'm going to dance again and find joy in my life."

I made my way back home. My list was waiting to be checked off. I walked in and all was as well as it could be. I filled a glass and began gulping it down. I had this agreement with myself to drink a cup of water before having coffee or soda. Therefore, cutting my addiction to caffeine in half.

Halfway through the glass, I was startled and spilled water down the front of my shirt. The dogs started barking in full force letting me know we had a visitor. Sophie, excited, ran out of her room. "Dad's here! Dad's here!" She often waited for him to come back home. It was heartbreaking to watch most days.

My heart sank and tears welled up. I pushed it all down and smiled. A tear trickled down anyway, so I ran to the bathroom. Grabbing toilet paper, I dabbed my eyes quickly. I looked into my own eyes in the mirror, "Katy, you are strong. You can do this. Don't you let him see one tear. Force that smile on your face! Life's just fabulous!" This made me laugh and so I began to naturally feel better. I put my head up, straightened my shoulders, smiled, and walked out of the bathroom.

I found Sophie sitting on the couch with her dad. She was explaining to him all about the counselor fiasco. He nodded lovingly at her and simply said, "I'm sorry that happened. We will find someone else." Sam walked over to the freshly made pot of coffee and filled his to-go cup and turned around. "Hey, can we talk in my office?" I found enough courage to look him in the eyes without crying. I noticed his look. The one he gives when something bad has just happened. "Sure," I answered.

We went to the "office," where we could talk "privately." It was outside in a shed we had purchased shortly after building our home.

When I walked in, Sam was already sitting by his desk in the office chair. "What's going on? I can tell you are upset about something." He looked at the floor and explained that he didn't have his most recent position anymore. I really felt like I could faint at that very moment.

Sam was paying the house payment, though he had already moved out. I was paying all the smaller bills with an $11 an hour paycheck and driving 30 minutes each way. I was struggling… with a second or third job, I couldn't make the money he was making… We already had land on the market from our farm. Even if the land sold at our price, it wouldn't cover our home.

I was furious… All the emotions boiled up again and tears began streaming. I was heartbroken and angry. I was furious with Sam, his young whore… and God. I started picking up things and throwing them on the other side of the shed. Oh, I wanted to throw it all at him, but I didn't. Instead, I threw it around our side-by-side. Empty plastic buckets, tools, papers, signs. Anything I could get my hands on.

I eventually stopped, exhausted. I don't remember Sam's exact words, but basically the realtor would call me. Vanessa had talked with me many times about selling our precious land and home. What Sam and I had worked and saved together for 20 years was disappearing in a moment.

Previously, I had fought against it. I wanted to save what I could and not move both kids right now as they had been through enough. Adam was finishing school and I was trying to protect him as best I could. Sophie loved her dad and didn't want to comprehend him moving out and in some ways she couldn't.

I may have been "just a mom and wife," but I worked just as hard. He would not agree, however. I knew that. He was always reminding me how he sacrificed himself to support us. I merely raised the children, homeschooled, and kept up with the home. After time went by, he had forgotten that Soph and I almost died the day of her birth. He denied the truths of the cyst on her brain. It was my fault she somehow couldn't develop as fast as her peers. In his eyes, "I had let myself go and complained too much."

Vanessa called that evening and said she would be over in a day or two to look around and take pictures. I agreed and attempted to sound brave. Putting the phone on mute while she talked, I was sobbing.

After talking to the realtor, I called my mother. I gave an account of the events that unfolded later that day. My mom was going through all of this with me. We cried together. She was hurting and heartbroken, too. She felt my pain and her grandchildren's pain, too.

When I went to bed that night, I didn't pray. What was the use? God wouldn't hear me anyway. He didn't care. If he did, we wouldn't be in this mess.

A few weeks later, we were piling all our things into the biggest truck we could rent. The kids and I could only take what would fit. I told myself to be grateful. At least I got to keep some of my things. It's most important the three of us and our two little fur babies would all be together. I wondered how it was all going to work. Living with my parents wasn't going to be easy for any of us.

They were used to living as a couple for several years now. We weren't used to Sam being gone. Now another change ensued. I couldn't spend too much time thinking about it. I didn't know how I could get through it if I focused on it too much. So, I just had to go through the motions.

It only took a few hours. The house was empty. What we couldn't fit, went into our storage unit; most of my son's collections and a few pieces of furniture, some of my daughter's things, and our previously stored belongings. We hadn't even had time to move in all the way when chaos began.

I couldn't walk through the house. It was too traumatic and painful. My car and my mother's were filled up with part of what we had left. I was so grateful for the family that helped us and were already on the way in a few other vehicles along with the moving truck.

The kids hugged their dad and got in the car. It didn't register for us that we wouldn't come back home this time. Eerily, it felt like we were going for a visit. How could we even process leaving the hometown we loved for good?

I stood there and looked at him. I couldn't hold it in any longer. I sobbed. I wasn't angry at that moment. I was grieving. I still loved who he was. I grabbed him and hugged him as tight as I could and said that I loved him. Sobbing, I said, "But you were my best friend." What I couldn't get out were a series of questions. How can you do this? What about your kids? How do you devastate your family that you are supposed to love and cherish?

I wasn't understanding. Like my daughter, I couldn't comprehend it.

It was like a nightmare I couldn't shake myself awake from. The tears and crying came from deep in my soul. What was left of it. I told him I loved him with all my heart. It was a cry I don't ever remember experiencing in my life. One you may only express on the death bed of a loved one.

He hugged me back and I could tell his eyes welled up with tears, too. I don't remember his exact words at that moment, but he gently asked me to calm down. "Take care of my babies for me," he began to sob. I replied, "You know I will always take care of them with everything I have."

I pulled myself together as I sat in my car taking deep breaths and holding it. My body shaking, from the sorrow within. I wondered how I was going to make the six-hour trip. Already having severe anxiety when driving, this seemed like an impossible mission. I took another deep breath in and reminded myself that we had to leave. The situation had become unbearable. The house must be sold.

The trip was daunting and longer than normal. We stopped several times. There was the normal restroom and food breaks for us and the dogs. Also, extra stops for me when anxiety crept up. My whole-body tense and aching, I wasn't sure if I had the strength left after such an exhausting and emotional morning. Well, really months. I knew I had to do it. There was no option even if this was the first time I had ever driven this far.

Finally, we pulled into the driveway at dusk. It had been a long seven-and-a-half-hour drive. On the bright side, we were all overjoyed to be "home." My dad was waiting on the front porch with his sweet smile. Greeting us and ready for hugs. I have never been so glad to see my father in all my life. I wanted to melt, for him to hold me like a little girl, and make everything better again. I wished it was that simple and gave him the tightest hug.

Our new home was in North Carolina, my parents retired there several years ago. My dad always wanted to live at the beach. So once my mother retired, they headed out to paradise. I was thankful they made this decision now.

We began unpacking the car before collapsing into bed. Tomorrow we will have the moving truck to unpack. I reminded myself once more that everything was going to be ok.

I brought in my box and shut my bedroom door. I opened it up. It was still safe inside. It was the last gift Sam gave to me. Now I wonder if he wanted me to use it. Maybe then he would finally be free. He could keep everything and live his new life without the consequences of divorce. I wrapped it up tight in the old, tattered towel and placed it carefully in the closet.

I decided at this moment to leave my box in the closet up high. Safe and sound forever. "I'll ride solo from now on," I thought.

The next morning the moving truck and our loving family came to help us split our things between my parents' garage and a storage unit. We were all fast and efficient. There was still a 6-hour trip back to Virginia for some.

We said our goodbyes and gave huge hugs. I wondered when we would see everyone again. We hadn't lived in another state from most of our loved ones before. We wouldn't be able to make a 30-minute drive down the road and visit.

After the goodbyes and hugs were delivered all around, I decided to take a walk on the beach. It was long overdue.

The wind was blowing through my hair and whipping my face as I walked. I was smiling as the salt air tickled my nose and stuck to my skin. I felt relieved. For now, it is over. I could breathe for a moment.

In some ways, I was excited about moving to the ocean. I didn't know how long I was going to stay or what the future held for us. To my surprise, Sophie and Adam were happy and relieved too. The burden of the last few years was rough on everyone.

This time I decided to write something joyful. Sitting in my chair, I dug my heels into the sand. I let the warm sand engulf both feet to the ankles. I folded my towel into a neat rectangle and placed my notebook on top. I grabbed a pen and began to write:

"Living The Life I Imagine"

I pictured
My life
A certain
Way.
The road

Was concrete
And would never
Be broken.

Suddenly,
The highway
Ended.
I was abruptly
Thrown out
Into the brush.

I was bruised
And broken.
The perfect
Road
Had vanished.

My head
Was a raging
Storm.
Tornadoes were
In my eyes
Swirling.

The world
Was spinning
Too fast
For me to
See.

Healing was long
And messy.
However,
I learned
To dig out
The yucky
Places.

Using a shovel,
I cleared out
The mud
And muck
Of my mind.

Sometimes
I watched
The huge mound
Fall back into
The blackness.
Tears flowing,
I kept digging.

I never
Gave up
Emptying
The old.
Consistency
Is Key.

Continuing
To dig,
I began
To fill up
With what
I desire
To be.
The new soil
Is rich
And abundant.
Infused with
Love,
Joy,
And Peace.

I love myself
Deeply.
I'm greeted
With sweet
Fragrant thoughts
Of gratitude
Each morning.

Now I cruise
On a quiet
Country road.

Rocky and worn,
The path is

Bouncy.
However,
The surprises
Are what
Keeps life
Fun and exciting.

As I travel,
I smile brightly.
The view
Is stunning
With hardwoods
And wildflowers
Decorating
The sides
Of the road.

Occasionally,
I slow down
To gaze at
The deer,
Turkeys,
And squirrels
As they stroll
Across my path.

No longer
In fear,
I am deciding

To get back
On the
Highway.

I am thrilled,
As I shift
To the journey
Ahead.
Intuition
Is whispering
The way.

The scenery
Is now
Melting away.
The hardwoods
And wildflowers
Disappear
And a bridge
Is in full view.

I joyfully
Make my way
Across.
A new painting
Emerging
Quickly
And easily.

I am beaming
As the sea
Greets me
And waves.
I smell and taste
The salty air
As it wafts
Into my window.
I watch the water
Chopping across
The sunlit
Horizon.
With a bump,
I return
To land.

The road
Leads to
A gorgeous
Cottage.
Her friend
Is the ocean
And they
Graciously
Invite me
To stay.

I walk in
And know

This is
My home.
I am smiling
From the
Inside out.

The feeling
Of gratitude,
Love,
Joy,
And Peace
Radiates
From my soul.

I am living
The life
I imagine.
Serving others.
Shining brightly
Being me.

I looked up at the waves again. Two seagulls were watching with me and hoping I might have a snack. I grinned as the little sandpipers were rushing down to the water and grabbing their dinner. Back and forth they would scurry in, grab, and go before the salt water rushed in to steal their evening meal. I shut my eyes and took a deep breath. Finally, a moment of peace.

Kathryn Simpson Baskette

K aty Baskette was born in a tiny dot of a town of south central Virginia. She has been an author since she could form words.

Her passion is poetry which is her way of connecting with God. It also serves as an outlet, a therapy to sort out and rid herself of life's pains and struggles.

Katy was married for 20 years which blessed her with two wonderful children. She homeschooled them both for over 16 years and proudly watched them graduate from high school.

The chapter Katy wrote in this book is a mixture of poetry and the story of her hardest moments in life.

Originally, Katy thought she should give the reader a more positive and healing part of her journey. However, she felt the calling to share the darkest part of her life once her pen started flowing on the paper.

After all, if we don't know darkness, how can we know light?

Today, she has continued healing and wishes to serve others that have gone through similar situations. She also wants to share that in her present chapter of life Katy is walking in courage and confidence following her purpose. She has found peace and gratitude daily even on the harder days. Her goal is to write more poetry and stories to publish.

The treasures she has written in secret and stored away will trickle out and shine one by one. Katy desires to spread love, joy, and peace to all through her writing.

Finding Growth Through A Pandemic
Kendra Kautz

This is for anyone who has been struggling, really in any aspect of life, but maybe you have a chronic health condition, maybe you suffer from anxiety or depression or you don't feel you have a handle on your life in general. I write from a place of honesty and want to provide some education in hopes to be of service for whomever resonates with my story.

We all have had times of struggle, regardless of how big or small, it matters that the feelings around the struggle impacted you. My goal is to be up front and open up about situations that I've gone through and share the life and health lessons I wish I knew earlier...

To begin, I'm a chiropractor based in Orange County, Ca and I've made it my goal to educate my patients (or anyone who cares to listen); your body is resilient and can heal if you have the right tools supporting it.

Although I was treated by a chiropractor since I was a baby, I don't think I was a true believer in holistic medicine until recent years because I was so ill growing up. I thought feeling like absolute shit (pardon by French) was the baseline for how everyone felt. Having a headache, bloating, or intestinal pain was a part of my everyday life until college.

I struggled with various other symptoms from psoriasis to recurring bacterial infections where my primary care physician would try to send me home with medication after a 15 minute visit where nutrition or my mental state was never addressed.

I spent countless hours in orthopedic surgeon's offices and in physical therapy clinics trying to recover from 4 knee surgeries that I now believe were all preventable.

I spent a good portion of my mid 20s trying to figure out why I was always so tired, irritable, mildly depressed, and overall, physically depleted from being in pain.

I thought taking 6-8 Advil a day was normal. I believed that if I had a bacterial infection I needed to take antibiotics. If I had a cold, I would take Nyquil. I hate to admit this, but I never believed that I was in control of my health. I really fell into the victim role of my circumstances because I was given very little direction or education on how to find a resolution.

This isn't to blame anyone along my journey, because education around health really didn't ramp up until our recent global crisis with

COVID-19. I also encountered many intelligent people along the way who did help me to some extent, most of whom were chiropractors, but I don't think all of the puzzle pieces around my health came together until I attended chiropractic school myself.

You know how people say, you typically go into a health profession if it's something you need help with? This was me without realizing it - I needed the chiropractic and holistic education for myself just as much as I needed it to help my future patients.

As a child I was consistently out sick with strep throat, ear infections, colds, flus, headaches, or stomach aches. It got to the point of occurring so often I really didn't know what it felt like to be well. Being sick was my normal.

When I was in class I could barely remember words I just read and I always had trouble focusing in class. I missed so many days of school when I was younger due to being sick that I vividly remember a teacher telling my mom I might need to be held back so I could catch up.

School became something I just wasn't interested in unless it had to do with sports. Any sort of activity came naturally to me so sports became "my thing". School fell by the wayside because at that time I was very uninterested in focusing on something I wasn't good at. This really led to me believing I wasn't smart. I grew up feeling I wasn't enough, outside of sports.

Little did I know that I was actually suffering from brain inflammation that caused me to lack focus, learning ability, and memory from poor gut health. I know so many children and adults suffer with the same frustrations today, so we will touch more on that later.

Jumping forward to high school, where all my focus still remained with sports, I tried out for the soccer team and phew, we made it! Not too long after my first high school season ended I sustained an injury in a recreational league game. Unfortunately, this initial injury turned into a cascade of injuries and then four knee surgeries. I remember feeling like I wasn't a "fast healer". Any injury I sustained just seemed to last forever, until I eventually gave up playing soccer. Even giving up the sport I loved so much didn't end the pain I was in all through high school and into college. I thought my knee pain was permanent from then on.

Now I know these injuries could have been prevented or healed faster, which once again, I will touch on more later.

Let's fast forward to freshman year of college, I'm having a freaking blast at Arizona State University because who doesn't when you attend that school. My mom is telling me how she's started to vomit after most meals and doesn't know what's wrong. She gets some lab work done and it turns out she has something called Celiac's disease. She begrudgingly tells me she thinks I may have the same issue, since we learned it's hereditary and like I mentioned I always struggled with a headache, stomach ache, brain fog, bloating, or you name it.

So soon after being introduced to my new freedoms of having beer and late night pizza while running wild with my friends (I kid - beer is nothing to write home about), I gave up gluten and my whole world changed. I thought - holy crap, I can think! I can read! I feel good! Wow, I'm actually kind of smart!

I didn't realize my lack of focus and my inability to learn easily was stemming from this inflammation. With this realization of "oh hey, I am smart, so I can apply myself now" I decided I could attend graduate school if I wanted - so I transferred to University of Arizona (bear down) to finish out my undergrad where I studied pre-med but ultimately graduated with a journalism degree. This ultimately, after a turn of events and a few career changes, led me to chiropractic school.

I kept thinking, look at me go! I have this new confidence within myself knowing that I can get a doctorate.

Through chiropractic school, I was taught by an amazing mentor who introduced me to the practice of applied kinesiology, although he put his own spin on it.

And for those that have never heard of Applied Kinesiology, which is different from the study of Kinesiology, it's a system that evaluates structural, chemical, and mental aspects of health using manual muscle testing and other standardized methods of diagnosis. This system is more widely used by chiropractors, but is now being observed by dentists and other types of doctors and healers to evaluate and treat a person's wellbeing.

And despite the negative information you might find on Google about it, it was the only system that worked to help me heal my health issues. This type of hybrid method that my mentor, Dr. Steve Schaffer used to evaluate and treat me was the only thing that made sense for my health history and chronic injuries.

Through this evaluation, you assess dysfunction by tracking imbalances back to the nerve root. If you have a segment of your spine that is always out of alignment, you can identify what muscles and organs that nerve root controls and see if the issue lies in those areas before blaming the spinal misalignment on structural fault alone. It's important to realize that someone can have a chemical misalignment of the spine, less known as a visceral somatic subluxation or deafferentation. This chemical misalignment happens when an organ is overworking so it causes a nervous system overload and breakdown, almost like when there's an electrical break in a circuit.

This type of evaluation has really served me and my patients, especially those suffering from chronic misalignments and those who have been adjusted over and over without much improvement. These types of misalignments typically call for a change in diet or require a supplement to help jumpstart the organ system(s) that has "short circuited".

Once the corresponding organ is supported properly, the body settles, the mind settles, the spinal alignment holds - it's quite wonderful! Once I was taught this connection, I was able to correlate my health history with which internal organ systems may have needed more support along the way.

Once I changed my diet and supported myself correctly, my moodiness went away. I would no longer ruminate on long car rides, but instead look around me and appreciate my life. I was able to hold my chiropractic adjustments so my knees wouldn't take the grunt of my pelvic misalignments. I discovered my chronic misalignments were due to lack of proper nutrition and mental stress. The stresses from nutrition, mental stress (perfectionism), and my perception of things were causing my stress hormone (cortisol) levels to become dysregulated which would cause my high and low feelings.

For those wondering what someone suffering from this looks like. I was tired in the mornings and more awake at night. I would rely on bad foods or candy to keep me awake and functioning throughout the day. I was irritable, had poor muscle recovery, and would sometimes feel light headed if I got up too quickly.

I learned there are different phases of this chemical dysfunction which require different types of supplemental support, but the overarching thing that helped me feel better (and may help you, too) was focusing on veggies, potatoes, and fruits. A LOT of fruit. When our bodies are stressed, our bodies exhaust glucose stores so it's important to have an intake of healthy glucose. Mind you, this was for my specific case, however, I do feel that this focus for eating helped the majority of my patients with various conditions.

So once I graduated from chiropractic school in December of 2019, I was excited to share my knowledge and help as many people as possible! I finally got my license in the mail in March of 2020… and we all know what happened next. The world shut down, offices closed, and as most of us experienced, people were fearful of being around others.

As a brand new doctor out of school, I had my confidence rocked again as my views for how to best support my immune system were vastly different from others. Trying to navigate through this time of confusion really forced me to come into my own.

Thankfully I was already on such a high from feeling better health wise coming into our lockdown, but with health being the topic of most conversations during this time I was obsessive about learning & reading more on a daily basis. As I kept learning more and amplifying my health practices for myself and for patients I consistently wondered, why aren't there any preventative health tips being shared for people on the news? Why are we only talking about face masks, hand sanitizer, & distancing ourselves?

Through this time we all experienced the division of our communities: including families, friends, co-workers, spouses, and even strangers. It was crazy to observe screaming matches between strangers at stores. I was told several times I was irresponsible, selfish, and ill-informed for choices I made.

When it came time to make the decision of getting vaccinated or not, I already had minor cases of COVID two times and I was the healthiest I had ever been in my life. So when anyone told me I needed this in order to keep others safe, it made zero sense to me.

I also knew how viruses replicated from my recent studies in school, and when someone would tell me I was going to hurt someone else with my decision, when I knew very well how to keep my germs to myself, it once again, didn't make sense.

Despite my subconscious mind occasionally allowing old beliefs to surface pertaining to my intelligence, I stood strong behind my education and reasoning.

I would respond to people questioning me with, "it's my job to help people, to keep them healthy and thriving - why would I ever want to do something that could potentially hurt my patients or anyone for that matter?"

This is the truth I've always led with, through this time. I did not think I needed to get a vaccination when I felt in my heart I was healthy and my choice will not affect others.

On the other hand, I would say the majority of people in my close circles were not in agreement with me. I respected their choices, but mine were not met with that same grace.

Unfortunately one of my biggest challenges arose when my brother and I didn't see eye-to-eye on this topic. I respected his fears and reality through this tough time on how to best keep his family safe, but our differences of opinion turned into unproductive emotional dialogue back and forth which led to the final decision that I needed to stay away from his family.

I understood the decision.

Did I like it? No. Did I agree it was the best way to keep them safe? No.

The overwhelming emotions I felt from this disagreement and division of our family was really the catalyst for me to have the most personal growth. I decided I needed to learn to take responsibility for myself, my actions, and my emotions. Afterall, my brother and I were the type of siblings that never fought. From day one, he had my back and I had his. I think we always had a mutual respect for one another despite how different we may have been. I always described my brother to others as a saint because he is - he's the most wonderful person I know and it broke my heart that someone I loved so much was so hurt by my actions and didn't want to see me anymore.

I had to constantly remind myself that these choices my family made were not something that I can control or convince them otherwise. I knew if I couldn't control my reactions and emotions to the events happening around me, I would suffer.

So I set out with a game plan to let the situation go and not allow it to affect my energy. I was already studying a useful tool called RTT hypnotherapy by Marisa Peer who teaches people how to rewire old subconscious beliefs from childhood. It was eye opening to examine why certain situations or other's actions would trigger me. I began deep diving into meditation practices to change the chemical stress response in my body, which led me to learn more from Joe Dispenza & Bruce Lipton. I would listen to recordings of Abraham Hicks, the spirit who speaks through Esther. Abraham's message is all about the law of attraction and how what we energetically put out in the world is what we get back. I started to evaluate all aspects of my life and realized if I wasn't getting what I wanted out of life, I needed to adjust my internal state to attract the quality outcome I was looking for.

Deep diving into these practices caused me to examine how I handle all areas of life - my romantic relationships, my work, my parents, my friendships, and most importantly my relationship with myself.

Having this disagreement with someone I idolized ever since I could remember, who questioned me and my beliefs when I knew deep down that my intentions were pure, truly made me buck up, stand up for myself, and build a confidence I've never had before to step out on my own.

And through this self exploration, here are 10 lessons I found extremely valuable when my energy needed a shift:

1. Instead of trying to understand someone's actions, focus inward to better understand yourself.

2. How you are feeling is completely up to you, not what others do or don't do for you.

3. We are in control of our reality and if someone isn't in alignment with yours, we can't expect others to get on board.

4. Defensiveness does not serve you, neither does justification.

5. Blaming a situation for your unhappiness gives away your power.

6. Shift your mindset away from crisis as that gets you nowhere.

7. Don't feel guilty for feeling blissful in times of crisis. You're more likely to help from a state of happiness versus crisis mode.

8. Dimming yourself or your light doesn't help others feel less insecure.

9. It's not selfish to put yourself first if you are working to be in a happier place as that eventually serves people more.

10. Leading with love is really the only way out of a difficult situation.

I found all these lessons can be applied to any situation. I think we are quick to become defensive or judge others when we are internally struggling. It's useful to acknowledge your response to things, may require some internal reflection versus outward projection.

Specific to how COVID-19 affected the world, can't we all just acknowledge it was a time led with a huge question mark and everyone was struggling?

And isn't it more productive to meet everyone with grace and understanding instead of anger and disapproval?

I think that deep down we all tried to do our best (and generally do), so those who were scared, rude, or isolated probably needed the most love.

As someone who works to improve the health of people, I think learning to be responsible for what you put out, energetically and physically is the first step in healing. It all starts with belief that you can get better, then feeling that internally, and not allowing outside influences or sabotaging beliefs to create your reality.

Step two is identifying root cause stressors which may have caused your symptoms, but the money is in the mindset. Once your body has reached a state of internal peace and nervous system regulation, internal dysfunctions can alleviate themselves more efficiently.

Most importantly, step three is to enjoy all the ups and downs of what you are bringing into your life and know that every up or down serves a purpose. The key is to allow things to happen and trust the process.

Kendra Kautz

D r. Kendra Kautz is a chiropractor and holistic health consultant in Orange County, Ca. Her personal health history of experiencing burnout, GI issues, brain fog, poor immune function, numerous injuries, and surgeries has led her to practice the way she does today.

She uses applied kinesiology, cranial sacral techniques, RTT hypnotherapy, and functional medicine to diagnose and treat each patient as a whole person.

Dr. Kendra understands the body will not perform optimally if there is dysfunction structurally, chemically, or emotionally. She spends the time educating her patients on how these dysfunctions affect their overall health and involves the patient in their healing process.

When she isn't treating patients, she enjoys going to the beach, playing volleyball, group exercise (spin, yoga & strength classes), hanging with her dog, and learning the latest and greatest at seminars!

Contact info:
@doctor_kendra
drkendrakautz@gmail.com
doctorkendra.com

You Are the Medicine
Jenn Maroney

I'm here, I'm listening. I love you."

Attending one of my very first breathwork sessions, I repeated these words over and over again in my mind as I rocked back and forth sitting crossed legged on the floor. I brought my knees up to my chest and squeezed my body into itself. Hot tears were streaming down my face uncontrollably as I allowed those words to hit deep down into my system. I knew that everyone was watching me, and maybe in another time I would have been mortified to be seen in this way. Vulnerable. Emotional. Unhinged. The "old" me would have died seeing this display of weakness being offered in front of so many people. But in this moment, with my own arms wrapped around me, I couldn't care less what anyone thought about my emotionality. The tears that were falling from my eyes and landing on my tattered blue sweatshirt seemed like years of broken promises, disappointments, and heartbreaks. They fell slow and intermittent at first, but as the music took a crescendo and the guide spoke the words, " I've got you, I'm not going anywhere," it was like the jenga blocks I had built around my heart all came tumbling down, and I wailed from a place deep within me that I didn't even know existed. Feeling so seen and held in that moment, the guide pulled the final piece that broke down the wall. This was me - and I was finding my way home to myself - one breath at a time.

I used to think I could mindset my way out of anything. In a world where everyone is a Mindset Coach teaching you "change your thoughts, change your life," I felt like I was missing the mark. I would stand in front of the mirror night after night, repeating powerful mantras like, "you are powerful" and "you are worthy of all you desire," and I would feel like a complete fraud. Like trying to fit a square peg into a round hole, it just wasn't working for me. I signed up for all the classes offering key principles of loving yourself, bought every book I saw someone recommend on social media about "living your best life" and prayed to God that these tools would offer me relief from my internal torment, this nagging feeling in my gut that something was wrong with me. These things never really worked, except providing a momentary glimmer of hope - but it never lasted longer than a few days before I fell back into old habits and emotions. The repeated disappointment of yet again feeling like I was falling short just left me defeated. A downward spiral of negative thoughts sucked me into my mind and I wondered if I was broken. At the time, I didn't realize that my body was such a wise soul, and as much as I tried to positively affirm my way into radical self-love and acceptance - she could not be manipulated by my words. My body knew how I was speaking to myself night after night, and the physical and emotional abuse I was putting it through. As much as I tried to fake it - the confidence, the worthiness, the self-love; my body KNEW that I had work to do. True transformation was never going to come by changing the clothes I wear, or fixing my hair - I was being called up to do ROOT work.

On the outside my world looked picture perfect; I had the husband, the great career, the house, all the makings of an amazing life. But on the inside I was scared, unhappy, insecure, and drinking more nights than not to escape my reality; I was a public success and a very private failure. I so desperately just wanted to be seen, to feel good in my own skin, and to be loved. Instead I felt like I was out in the middle of the ocean, being pulled under by the current, and I was grasping for someone or something to save me. I sought out anything that could possibly bring an end to the tumultuous ocean of emotions happening within me. I was constantly chasing the dopamine hits to keep me from drowning, but the high was short lived, and I would wind up bruised and beaten down by my own actions and decisions. I lived in this pattern for many years, waking up each morning asking myself, "how the fuck did I get here?"

Isn't it funny that somewhere in our storyline we get this feeling that it's just not OK to show up in our "US-NESS?" Maybe it's not one specific time that you can recall, maybe it's just small micro experiences that slowly have chipped away over time to this point now, where you feel completely unrecognizable to yourself. And so you decide that it's maybe safer, easier even, to be something different - something more desirable - to fit in. To be liked. To be like a chameleon.

I've worn so many masks throughout my life I could supply an entire masquerade ball. One of my earliest memories of this was the day my mom drove me away from my childhood home because she was divorcing my dad. It was in that moment where I came to understand that sometimes people will lie to make others feel better. As I looked out the back mirror, my mom encouraged me to sit down in my seat and turn around. I remember her telling me "It's ok Jennie. We are just going on a little trip, like a vacation." As I turned around and flopped in my seat, cheeks red and swollen from crying, it's like I knew that my life was changing forever, but my little being just couldn't grasp what was fully happening. So I put on my "be a big girl" mask, stifled the tears that were trying to escape my puffy eyes, and lowered back into my seat leaving my father in that rear view mirror. I didn't realize it at the time, but this was my very first heartbreak, and the moment in my life that would change me forever. Even at the young age of six, I felt this nudge to be strong for my mom, and not to make things harder than they already were. So I shoved the feelings deep down into the pit of my belly - the place that would soon be my own treasure chest of suppressed emotions waiting to be excavated.

I continued to abandon myself as the years went on, getting lost in bad relationships, an unhealthy relationship with food and my body, and really just putting myself in situations that didn't seem to be the real me - whoever that was, I wasn't even sure anymore. I wanted to be like the popular girls in high school, wearing the newest fashions and catching the eyes of the boys, so I would wake up two hours before school to prepare: a scalding hot shower to scrub my skin to a shine and shave my legs all the way up, and then cake make-up on my face and curl my hair. I would scrounge through my closet, dismayed that I didn't have Holister or Abercrombie to choose from, but would end up with the basic fitted tee and tight jeans. I was uncomfortable. The clothes were snug and the jeans were cutting into my stomach - but this was the look. So I sucked in, stood up tall, and wore the flirtatious smile that made everything OK. I deprived myself of lunch almost every day, in an attempt to just be "smaller" - only for the other girls to tease me about my clothes not fitting and commenting how my make-up didn't match my skin tone. I would go home and spend hours in front of the mirror, dissecting every single imperfection on my face, pulling at my skin and wishing that I could just be different - because ME wasn't enough.

This pattern of self-contempt continued through most of my adulthood, and I found myself chasing after anything that would temporarily mask the pain I was feeling inside. I would betray my own boundaries out of fear that someone wouldn't like me, and I often put myself in harmful situations for a momentary thrill that would only leave me feeling more defeated when it was over. I chased success, I chased love, I chased people, and I chased happiness - without once stopping to think about how this chasing was only taking me further away from me - MY truth, and MY medicine that was within me just waiting to get my attention.

I think a part of me always knew that living my life in this way wasn't sustainable, and eventually I would have to face my years of numbing, self-sabotage, and running from my emotions. You can only keep up the facade for so long, before it all comes crashing down. All my years of chasing after something to fill the void inside of myself had finally caught up to me, as I climbed out of my parents gray minivan on an appropriately cold and gloomy February afternoon; I found myself at a crossroads. I'm holding back the tears, trying to remain strong, more for my mom than for myself. I wrap my arms around her and breathe her in. I don't want to forget that scent. It's funny how a smell can immediately take us back to a moment in time... a memory... a person... I silently pray as I take a deep inhale that this smell will carry me through the next thirty-nine months. I feel her body trembling as I hold her tighter and she cries into my hair, words I cannot totally comprehend, but I catch the most important part - "I love you."

And then in what felt like a blink of an eye, a homely looking middle aged woman pulls up in what looks like a bread truck and orders me to get inside. I hug my mom a little tighter one more time, tell her that I will be fine and not to worry. With a final kiss on the cheek I look over at my stepdad and give him an apologetic look that says what I cannot get out of my mouth "I'm sorry to put you through this - please take care of her." He gives me a nod and a wink, and I start to walk away. I turn back around, muster up a smile and say, " just look away Mama, you don't need to see all this, I love you and it's going to be OK... I'm sorry for everything."

I walk towards the unfriendly looking officer, willing one foot in front of the other. "Don't look back, Jenn, don't look back." I know that if I did that I would collapse. Tears would consume me and I would run back, wishing to just crawl up in my mom's lap and be held - go back to simpler times, before I allowed my life to become such a mess, a time before this exact moment - where I'm about to spend 39 months of my life in federal prison. As the truck door slams behind me, I'm shackled at my hands and feet, connecting to my waist - I raise my eyes up to God and pray for the strength I know I will need to get through this chapter of my story. At this moment I know I have a choice - Will I allow this chapter of my life to merely be another "thing" that happened on my timeline? Something I would cling to as part of my identity that would just continue to give rise to feelings of insecurity, failure, and unworthiness? Or would it be different this time? There has to be a lesson in all of this madness - and although it's not completely clear to me as I hear the iron gates clank loudly behind me - I know it's coming. This is one of those crossroad moments - and I'm about to find out exactly why I am here.

As I lay my head down that first night, the sounds of hundreds of women sleeping all around me, I allowed just a couple of tears to fall down my face. Thirty nine months keeps repeating in my brain and I'm thinking I must be dreaming. This cannot be real. My entire life replays in my mind - my hopes, my dreams, and the famous line "how the fuck did I get here?" enters my mind once again. Before I even noticed my body moving, I was out of my metal bunk bed and found myself standing in a cold shower. Standing there in my nakedness, I begin slamming my fist into the concrete wall over and over again, until I finally see blood running down my arm onto the floor and circling down the drain. Even after everything that had gotten me to this point, I was still trying to push through the pain, the heartache, the sadness, without allowing myself the chance to actually feel what needed to be felt in my body in order to heal these old wounds bubbling up to the surface. When I was stripped away of all the "things" I had used to define myself as a person - the career, the husband, the house, the success - I had absolutely no idea who I was - and that reality was terrifying to me.

I remember standing in a room for one of my first group counseling sessions I was required to attend like it was yesterday. An older woman looked me dead in my eyes and said, "Your blind spot is that you're absolutely miserable inside, you hate yourself and you don't even see it. You have no idea who you are." I stood there in front of fifteen other women and I just froze. I couldn't move. I was so embarrassed? Angry? Ashamed? Or maybe I just felt **exposed**. In a matter of a few moments, this woman had stripped me to my core, and shined a light on the part of me I had tried to keep hidden for so many years. I spent so much of my life trying to be the "**good girl**," do the things I was supposed to do like get good grades, go to college, get a good job, get married - all the while I was drowning in my own thoughts and fears and felt miserable. Too afraid to speak up, to rock the boat, to show any signs of weakness. And here in this small room with all these eyes on me, I couldn't hide anymore. I was in prison. I had nothing left and I just stood there completely rocked. Cracked wide open. I calmly walked out of the room, trying to keep my composure - and then I sat in the bathroom stall and just quietly cried. I felt so completely broken.

Did everyone in my life know this about me too? How had I made such a mess of myself? I had never felt more hopeless. I had so much "stuff" to unpack, to heal, to discover about myself that led me to where I currently found myself - and I wondered if I would be able to make it. Will I be able to do this work? Could I survive this time away from everything and everyone I knew - and commit to re-writing my internal narrative?

That same woman came into the bathroom a few moments later, gently tapped on the door, and pulled me up off of the floor and into her arms, hugging me tightly, almost like a mother's embrace. She told me I had three choices - give up and just wait out my time, give in and allow this place to swallow me up, OR give it all I had and use these moments to heal the parts of me that need healing so I could go out and change the world. I don't think that woman even knows how much that day meant to me. How much it changed the trajectory of my life story. On that day, when totally exposed, she was a mirror to me, letting me know just what I was capable of doing with my life. I may not have created all the wounds but now it was my responsibility to heal them. Loving those parts of me that were hard to look at because they carried shame, disgust, anger, sadness, guilt, and regret. And looking at them with love rather than contempt. When I allowed myself to lean in with curiosity to those tender places, something magical happened for me. It was like a welcoming home.

Going to prison actually saved my life - and trust me when I say it has taken me a very long time to believe that statement as my truth. It was within those walls, where I finally met myself, the real me. I was surrounded by so much hurt and pain, not only my own, but hundreds of other women, who all had similar narratives - a need to feel seen, to be heard, to be loved. The pattern became so clear to me - the constant pattern of looking outside of ourselves to address the wounding felt within. When I got courageous enough to look within, I realized that everything I had been searching for was with me the entire time - I was the medicine I needed. The little girl inside of me - she wanted me to pay attention, she wanted me to speak kind words to her, she wanted me to wrap her in my love and let her know that she was safe. It's funny and also kind of sad as I sit back and think of all the times I felt like I was being abandoned and I was the one abandoning me over and over again. Within that prison cell, I committed to showing up for myself - to allow this mess to become my message to others. I had to feel everything that I had been suppressing for so many years, and finally get into dialogue with my body - not with a lens of contempt and frustration - but with pure love and curiosity. When I made the decision to start speaking the language of my body - I was finally able to BREATHE.

I believe everything that has happened in my life has led me to this exact moment, has made me the person I am today - and I'm damn proud of the woman I've become. Every life experience has led me to this place, and it's my mission to support women on their own journey to coming home to themselves - meeting all parts with love and compassion so they can ultimately expand in whatever direction they desire. I turned a painful experience into my purpose, and now I guide other women as they work toward "remembering" who they are at a core level, before the world got a hold of them and placed expectations on how they should show up each day. My goal is to teach women how to unapologetically own their voice, and to recognize that everything they need to heal from their darkness is within them. Everything else we find ourselves chasing after will ultimately result in feelings of unfulfillment and disappointment - because WE are the medicine.

I AM THE MEDICINE.

YOU ARE THE MEDICINE.

WE ARE THE MEDICINE.

It's time to allow ourselves the space to truly heal from our wounds and our pain. It's time to surrender our old ways of coping, to release the defense mechanisms we have acquired over the years, and at last be a witness to our emotions; honoring whatever arises. We have to feel in order to heal. Day after day, despite all of our negative self-talk and sabotaging behaviors, our bodies continue to show up for us. They keep air in our lungs and a heartbeat in our chest. They keep showing up for us, regardless of how we treat it.

The invitation is always there - to lean in and listen, to get curious, to heal, to LOVE - will you answer the call?

Jenn Maroney

With over 12 years' experience in the mental health field, Jenn has pivoted from the corporate setting of mental health and now focuses on Somatic Healing & Coaching where she strives to empower women to tap into their inner badass through mastering their mindset, ditching self-doubt and fear, and stepping in to their greatness! Her goal is to teach women how to unapologetically own their voice and to recognize that everything they need to heal from their darkness is within them. After going through her own healing transformations, she now guides other women as they work toward "remembering" who they are at a core level, before the world got a hold of them and placed expectations on how they should show up each day.

Anyone who works with Jenn is guaranteed a unique and customized experience. With her eclectic toolbox of skills in Neuro-Linguistic Programming, Hypnotherapy, EFT, TIME Techniques, Yoga, Reiki, strength training, mental health, and trauma informed breathwork she is prepared to create a personalized transformation.

IG: @iamjennmaroney
Website: www.jnmcoaching.com
Email: jnmaroney@gmail.com

My Scars Are Not Hidden
Zell McFail

My scars are not hidden, they are and have always been in plain sight. Though noticeable to all, they are unrecognizable to many. Most look at them from a surface point of view when in all reality the damage lies beneath. Looking at them one will believe that they may know the cause and the cure, but nothing can be further from the truth. Until we learn to get past the surface to the core, we will always call the scars what they are not. The funny thing about it is there are many that share the same scars and more like them, but they are not looked at close enough to be recognizable.

The scar of abuse, whether it be physical, mental, emotional, or sexual; is a scar. Neglect, heartbreak, being rejected by family, friends or foe, low self-esteem, death of a loved one, or whatever it may be; they all leave nasty, painful, unnoticeable, unrecognizable scaring. Unfortunately, by the time it surfaces it's too late, all the damage has been done. It kind of reminds me of a decubitus ulcer. You can see the red and swollenness on the outside of the skin but, the real problem lies beneath the skin.

As a healthcare provider for over twenty years, one of the many in-services that I've attended was concerning the decubitus ulcer or bed sore as it is most often called. A bedsore or decubitus ulcer is an injury to the skin and underlying tissue resulting from prolonged pressure on the skin. This sore starts from the inside and because of all the pressure from staying in the same space or place for a prolonged amount of time without repositioning, it eventually makes its way to the surface. Once on the surface, it is noticeable but not always recognizable; depending upon who has noticed it. In other words, you will have to know a little about bedsores to know if there is a problem that lies beneath the surface.

As the bedsore has now surfaced, it will take a lot of attention from a trained licensed healthcare professional or wound nurse to begin the healing process. At this time, the wound must be measured to see the depth of it to determine what kind of care is needed. I've seen numerous times that a wound vac must be used to remove some of the pressure, reduce swelling, and help clean bacteria from the wound to assist with the healing and closure of it. They call this wound therapy. Do you see my scars now?

For me, there isn't much of a difference between the process of a bedsore and the process of dealing with unresolved pressures of life. If we compared the two, we would find that they both cover how deep the pressure and pain is. As with decubitus, the unresolved pain of a person must be measured to see exactly what and how much care would be needed to begin the healing process. In some cases, the therapy must be handled aggressively. Low self-esteem has now set in along with darkness, anger, fear, and all manners of negativity; to trust another seems almost impossible and is far from the mind because of the pain that has already been afflicted on you by the person or persons.

Day after day you fight hard to stay alive, hoping and praying that someone will save you from this suffering. Days turn to nights, nights turn to weeks, weeks to months and then years but nothing. For some, dying appears to be the best and only way out and so they take their own life. A life that was filled with purpose and dreams that has now fallen prey to the wickedness of another.

I wonder, did you see their scars? Did you dismiss them for what you believed to be attention seeking or maybe you were one of the ones that added salt to the already injured. Could it be that you are one of those who says, "hurt people hurt people". My take on that statement is if you know the pain that it caused you and what it felt like to go through whatever it may have been; then how can you do those same horrible things to another? Again, this is just my opinion.

Now, can you see the scars?

Depression, loneliness, heartaches, pain and darkness; just to name a few.
Not to forget the physical, mental, and sexual abuse, too.
The desire to be loved or even recognized.
The heartbreak that is felt when you look into the accusers' eyes.

*Why are you doing this to me, do you not care? Of course, not, I say to myself, I
see your blank stare.*
Some were programmed to be quiet and leave the past behind.
For others like me, no peace I find.
I try to cover it up by being silent and pray.
*Most times that doesn't even help because I fall asleep not wanting to see the next
day.*

Surely you can see the scars now, but you were calling it something else. Junky, crackhead, lazy, whoremonger, Jezebel, morbidly obese, anorexic, crazy, severely depressed, PTSD, a recluse, and so many more adjectives that have been attached to them or shall I say, "us". In all reality, these things are not who we are, but they are the result of the real issues that lie beneath the surface. Issues that may have caused overindulging in food, sex, drugs, or alcohol. These issues do not only affect the parts that you see on the surface but also are known to cause stress that breaks down the immune system causing more trauma to the body and mind. Trauma such as stomach ulcers and Gerd, thyroid problems, high blood pressure, diabetes, asthma, heart disease, and even Alzheimer to name just a few. Do you see the scars?

Surely by now you're able to recognize what you've noticed. For some you will no longer view the surface and conclude, but now prayerfully your eyes have been opened and maybe you will look deeper. Others may willingly continue to be surface searchers because of the fear of the unknown or simply because of the fear of finding their own decubitus. I know they are there; I've seen them, I've lived them, and I know they aren't as hidden as you may think. How do I know, you may ask? Well, it's not because someone has told me but it is because experience has been my best teacher.

Good Morning

Each day has its own interruptions, problems, concerns, and troubles. For the most part, right now, all my days are pretty much the same. Upon opening my eyes each day, I whisper a prayer to my Lord up above. Worship has been a part of my daily life for a long time. I believe as the scripture says, "Seek ye first the kingdom of God." I believe sometimes that we get so caught up in the business of the world that we don't stop and give the Lord what he is due.

"Thank you & forgive me." I say thank you because God is kind enough to allow me to see another day and compassionate enough to allow me to get whatever my wrongs are, right. I say forgive me because at some point throughout the day more than likely there may be a chance that I may do something or say something that may not be pleasing in his sight.

Along with saying, "Thank you and Forgive me" I also recite the first verse in what is known as *The Lord's Prayer*, "Give us this day our daily bread". I recite this because I need the Lord of my life to give me what I may need for the day's journey because tomorrow is not promised to us. What will be my assignment for today? Who will you allow me to minister to or who will you allow to minister to me? I never know which way it's going to go from day to day but nevertheless it's in my will to allow the Lord to lead me.

Today I Cried

Today is one of those days that I mentioned before when I say, "No peace I find". Today I cried. I woke up in sorrow and disappointment. My day hasn't even begun, yet still I cried. No one said anything, no one did anything, no interruptions, no problems, no troubles or concerns but, a lot of tears and for what I had to ask myself. For some reason or another, a darkness had come over me like an overcast before a storm. My body is wrecked with pain, my eyes filled with tears, my stomach in a knot. I'm struggling to breathe. I feel like I don't want to breathe anymore.

My mind is flipping and I'm all over the place. It's hard for me to think clearly. I have but one thought and that is the thought of not being here anymore. So, with my eyes still closed, I stumbled from the prayer room where I fell asleep the night before to my office and I began to write, "Today I cried." Like many days or most of my days, today I cried. I cried because of the pain in my heart. It's been broken more times than I can count and by more people than I can think. I cried because of the wicked ways of the people in this world. I cried because it has been a long journey. A journey which I'm still unsure of. I cried remembering as far back as the age of six, I've carried the weight of the world on my shoulders. I cried because it appears that the things that I desire are far from me. I've never been hard to please but even still it feels as if the things that I long for are not likely to happen to me. I cried because I'm tired of my heart bleeding with pain and disappointment, heartaches and heartbreaks, setbacks and setups. I cried because there is so much death around me, so I cried. I cried because when thinking back over my life, I believe because of fear, I missed out on many opportunities. I cried because even at this late age, I feel there is no one to love me but God and him alone. I've tried repeatedly, but nothing. I cried because I'm just plain ole tired of things being the way they are. I'm tired of trying. Maybe death is the only way out. I'm tired of turning the other cheek. I'm tired of getting back on the horse after falling off. I'm tired of making lemonade after life gives me lemons. So, I cried. I'm tired of building a bridge and getting over it. I'm tired of trying again after not succeeding at first. So, I cried.

As I cried this morning, a song by the late Phylis Hyman rang out in my soul, "I can't stand this living alone." Can I tell you, I believe I can only imagine how she felt when she recorded that song. If it's anything like I'm feeling now, I pity her. So, I cried. I cried because I'm tired of hearing, "You'll be alright" but I'm not. I cried because I believe that some way or another, I'm always disappointing my Lord and savior. I cried because I want His perfect will for my life to begin to manifest but even in that, there are no signs; at least none that I can see or maybe there are but, the darkness has overtaken me. So, I cried.

I cried because I feel like all hope is gone. I cried because to me it's embarrassing as a minister to think the way I am thinking...hopeless. Where is the faith that I teach and preach about? I'm supposed to keep the faith no matter what the situation or circumstances may be, at least that is what I was taught. There is one bible scripture that comes to mind, "I have learned, in whatsoever state I am in, therewith to be content", says the Apostle Paul in Philippians 4:11. I just don't feel that way right now, so I cry. I can only think in my soul, "Will it ever get better for me?" It appears right now for me the title "Minister Zell" doesn't mean anything. It's difficult to apply scripture in this state of mind and believe me when I say, I know plenty of them. "Cast thy cares at the savior's feet for He cares for you", "We don't mourn as those that don't have hope", "Delight thyself in the Lord and He will give you the desires of your heart", "Look to the hills from which cometh my help", and many more scriptures from the Holy Bible right now does not do a thing for me.

I feel there is only but one light and that is the light that shall lead me up out of here. Help me Lord, please. Is there any help for me? I'm so numb right now.

Believe me when I tell you that I'm not living right now, I'm just existing. I can't lie this time, I'm not alright. Who besides God can I tell and who besides God may even care? Is there balm in Gilead to heal my soul? I don't know what else to do, so I cry. I don't know what else to pray for, so I cry. I am at the end of my rope. I can hope and pray that there is a "but God" to my story that will end all this madness. There has got to be a better end for me. I'm losing myself in this darkness. This is how I'm feeling this morning. I've heard it said many times before that a good night leads to a good morning. Can it be the reason why I'm feeling this way? Is it because last night my tears were my pillow? Is that the reason why I cry? I'm not sure but what I am sure of is, this morning like most mornings, I cried.

Happy Thoughts

When asked the question, "What is my happiest childhood memory?" I must admit for a brief second or two every part of my body stopped. I was stuck in a moment in time. Out of all the questions that have been asked about me, no one had ever inquired about my happiness as a child. They just assumed it was all good.

Although to some that question may have been a no brainer. For me, it was a hard and unwanted look back down memory lane. I had to revisit a past that had caused me much pain as a child and a lot of uncertainties as an adult. My mind was completely blank and a happy thought from my childhood was far from it.

As a child, one straight back ponytail was always the hairstyle of my choice and I always preferred ribbons over barrettes, dresses and skirts over pants, and tights over long socks. Green was my favorite color. I really didn't have a favorite type of shoe at that time. Now that I think about it, that's probably the reason why my mom always yelled at me about not having shoes on. She would say, "Girl put some shoes on them plantations".

Finally, I remembered the one time as a child I felt like I was on top of the world. It wasn't all bad; some days it just felt like it. For instance, the day I was to feel like I was important. It was the day I felt like God had smiled on me. I was in the first grade. My teacher was Mrs. Ogoroe. If my memory serves me correctly, she was a full-figured, pretty lady with beautiful, fluffy black hair. She was the best teacher I'd ever had. She was always so pleasant and nice to be around. She was one of those teachers that was willing to go that extra step to help her students. I believe she felt what we practice in this day, "no child left behind."

I watched her every move. I remember going home one day telling my mother that I wanted some crackers that you eat with the white stuff.

I didn't know then, but I found out later that the white stuff was cream cheese. I wanted it because I saw my teacher have it for lunch and I wanted to try it. It wasn't too long after that my mother got me the crackers with the white stuff and still to this day, I love crackers with the white stuff.

"Okay class, I'm going to play a new game with you", Mrs. Ogoroe said. "And the secret is in the middle." She started on the chalkboard and she wrote 6 _ 8. "What could that be?", I thought to myself.

After many tries from me and my classmates, it hit me. I raised my hand to be recognized and just like that, she bid me to come to the front. Being the shy person I am, I hesitated but then I worked up enough courage to walk to the front. As I walked up to the front with sweaty palms and little to no confidence, I noticed a smile on her face. She smiled as if she knew I knew the answer. I got close to her and whispered in a small still voice in her ear, "the secret in the middle is seven". "Yes, that's right and you get a star", Mrs. Ogoroe said. "I did it, I thought to myself." I'm important. I finally feel like I matter. I finally feel like this was a win for me and the best part is that no one could take it from me because no one else knew the answer but me. Finally, a victory that I didn't have to share. I answered first and it was all mine.

I'm Doing Fine

I've grown a lot in the last year and my faith has gotten stronger. Things are starting to look up for me now and I'm happy about it. One thing that I've learned during these troubled times is that tough times don't last but tough people do. I'm doing fine now, and I believe the best is yet to come. I'm gonna try my best to continue to look up; that is what real warriors do. My scars won't be the end of my story.

Zell McFail

Z ell Jaconda McFail is the Ceo and founder of the non-profit, Together We Win Corp. She is also a Bible Study teacher, Spiritual Guidance coach, personal caregiver, Staffing Manager, Minister and Mentor.

Zell's accomplishments include certification of completion in Bereavement Minister training, certification of completion in Management 101, Licensed Minister and Geriatric Nursing Assistance. As Ceo of Together We Win Corp, Zell holds bi-monthly support meetings for both men and women in a safe, and nonjudgmental environment. This corporation gave birth to Zell's first support group, "We Win". Since then, Zell has also joined with the "Uncensored Sisters" women's group.

As Minister and spiritual coach, Zell's passion is getting others to understand, acknowledge and walk in the powers that they possess within to live a life of freedom, wholeness, and balance unapologetically.

Caring for others is Zell's first love. Being able to care for her many nephews and nieces brings her great joy. Since the day Zell heard from the Lord, "Though you may not birth any, you will be mother to many," Zell never frets of being childless because, the Lord has given her many to nurture.

Email: Wewinningest2018@gmail.com
Email: Zell.McFail@aol.com

You Can Go From Here
Tammy T. Sapp

L adies, we can go on from here.

After the loss of my husband, my aunt, my uncle, and my mother, I did not think I could go on. I was numb for months. I sought counsel because I wanted to get out of the funk. I remembered Philippians 4:13, "I can do all things through Christ which strengthens me." I began to ask God for direction.

He directed me to Roberta's House. I met some great people to help me with this grief journey. I realized grief has no time limit. Also, I found out that everyone responds to grief differently. No longer do I listen to what I was taught. I was told not to question God about what happened, just keep it moving and time will heal it. Grief is a process so there are stages to it. Do not let anyone tell you differently. Grief is a normal response to loss during or after a disaster or other traumatic event. Grief can happen in response to loss of life as well as to drastic changes to daily routines and ways of life that usually bring us comfort and a feeling of stability. Common grief reactions include shock, disbelief, or denial. You are not alone. It is comforting to know that grief symptoms happen to everyone. It puts you on a healing pathway.

The path to healing from a loss is different for each person, one which may have unexpected twists and turns, but a road that has been traveled by many. No longer do I listen to what I thought grief was. I thought grief would be a quick response of sadness which I could get over easily. This time, losing my husband, my best friend, had me numb and feeling alone for the first year. I no longer respond and say I know how you feel when a loved one passes. I know how I feel but I do not know how it made you feel. Be patient with yourself. Do not compare yourself to others. Go through mourning at your own pace. Admit you are hurting and go with the pain. Ask for and accept help. Stop asking "Why? And ask "What will I do now? Know that you will survive. Take care of something alive, such as a plant or a pet. Schedule activities to help yourself get through weekends and holidays. Make sure you take care of yourself. Selfcare is not selfish. Rest and relax. Grief is an exhausting process emotionally. I get monthly massages and participate in breathworks. I was told that daily exercising can effectively control depression (the blues). It helps with my sleeping. Tears are a natural part of grief and they help relieve stress. Allow yourself to cry. Give yourself permission to release. Laugh, do not be afraid to. Just because you laugh does not mean that you are not grieving or missing your loved one.

There are special days in life such as birthdays, anniversaries, graduations, and weddings. They may be difficult days for the bereaved. They mean "family together", and it is currently that we are so acutely aware of the void in our lives. For many, the wish is to skip the day altogether. We may see the perfect gift for our loved one who has died and suddenly realize he or she will not seem possible, but grief will soften, and, with time and work, you will begin to enjoy life again.

Recipes for coping with a Special Day: R-IS FOR RITUALS REMIND INDIVIDUALS OF A SHARED BELIEF, E- IS FOR EXPRESS YOUR FEELINGS, C-IS FOR CONTROL THE DAY RATHER THAN LET THE DAY CONTROL YOU, I- IS FOR IMPORTANCE OF SELF-CARE, P- IS FOR PLAN AHEAD, E-IS FOR ENJOY!

I learned all these things from Roberta's House:
- SEEK HELP DON'T DO LIFE ALONE. Therapy is OK. Don't hold all your grief inside. This is for my family and friends: I want us to heal and be at peace with ourselves. Decide to take off that mask. Stop saying you are fine when you are not. Seek help and call on Jesus, I did. He never left us. He is the one that has carried us through our mess. Without our mess, there cannot be a message.

- GOD ALSO TOLD US TO TELL OTHERS. So share your stories and I know there is so much chaos and confusion all around but God will give you peace that will surpass all understanding. Remember it's your time! Take care of you! If you don't, you can't help anyone or live out the purpose God has for you.

Grief is a process so there are stages to it. Don't let anyone tell you differently.

Remember your loved one the way you want to. Do something that you and your loved one were supposed to do as a couple… finish the project. Go on a vacation, cross something off your bucket list. Let your loved one know you loved them and miss them.

Finish something your loved one was working on.

I finished the basement remodel. Right before our cruise in December 2021 our hot water tank went up two days before we left. That task took a long time to finish. Russ was supposed to handle it. I began getting estimates interviewed about nine contractors. I was looking for the person or persons to get the job done the way Russ would want. I asked my Wednesday night ladies group if they knew any one to do the remodel. Minister Moe said she knew of a person, Keith of K and L Contractors. The cave is Raven Purple with a black wood floor finish. Pictures of our favorite quarterback, Lamar Jackson, are pictured throughout. I have decided to mix some orange with the purple. Russ's favorite color was orange. The Orioles are doing excellent this year. I have to add them to the wall. I named it The Bird Town Cave, Ravens and Orioles.

Take the trip.

I took that first family trip without him and it felt different. It was well needed by everyone. I know Russ was there in spirit. We flew from Baltimore to Daytona Beach Florida. The hotel was beautiful, our little home away from home for those five days. Every morning I got up early, met the sunrise and the waves that came in like a roaring lion. It was so beautiful.

I know that my faith has wavered, but I will trust God. I give all praises to God for continuing to have my back. With his daily help you can do all things through him. Believe it or not, God has not forgotten about me. And here's how I know… I went to my first outing after my husband's death. I was quite numb. I was at a women's retreat. The name was If I Could Only Touch the Hem of His Garment. I believe that conference changed my life.

The first night was a meet and greet. The speaker was a widow about 18 months in. She was led to call all the widows to the front. I went up to the front and she asked me some questions. She asked me the question, "Do you need to scream or cry and let something out?" Yes, she was correct. I had not cried or screamed. I was in the first phase of grief, denial of the event that had taken place. After crying and screaming, I experienced such a great release. I started feeling like I could go on from here. I was told my pain has purpose. I had to go through this to birth this. There is life after death!

I began weekly sessions with my therapist because depression was trying to hold me hostage. I woke up one day and thought, I need to find myself. I had to keep reminding myself that I am an overcomer. I am a survivor and a believer. I reminded myself daily of what I have been able to overcome. I'm reminded of being a mother, sister, aunt, friend, and a prayer warrior even when going through all of this. I know I've been through a lot, but I survived. What did not kill me made me stronger. I started feeling I can go on from here.

Death comes in threes, I was always told. I had my bestie, my favorite auntie and two uncles pass the day before my 53rd birthday. I was numb again. We texted or talked. everyday. I really had to remind myself that I was a child of the highest, God. I can do all things through Christ.

I have endured so much loss this year but there's purpose in this pain. I carried the grief of the loss of my twins around for years, just dealing with it. No one ever told me about counseling. When you lose a loved one, it is like a piece of you died with them. Seeking help and weekly therapy sessions has helped me. Journaling has helped. writing your feelings on paper vs keeping them inside. I tend to be all over the place, grabbing one of my mini journals helps me to settle down. I find peace waking up early, putting God first by getting on the prayer line that I have been apart for over 27 years. I have witnessed our prayers being answered over and over.

The day Russ got sick it was January 5th. He woke up while I was getting dressed and said my "legs feel funny." I said, " Hunny, have a great day, see you later." I would usually get a call around lunch time but this day, no call. I called him, no answer so I just let him rest. I thought he would call when he got up. I got a call later around 3pm from my son saying "Mom, Dad called his brother here and he is unable to walk." They attempted to help him get up to get downstairs and it did not work. His brother called 911 at 3pm. I left work.. As I was riding home, I began to pray and ask God to do his will for my husband. I got to the house, and firefighters were still there waiting on an ambulance to come for Russ. They started oxygen and kept that going. A supervisor had to bring more because the fire truck was running low. I had never seen or heard of paramedics staying at a house for three long hours. The Pandemic and COVID numbers were up. A lot was happening. An ambulance showed up at 5:45pm. I made sure he had his charger so he could call us. The closest hospitals were full. They were taking him to UMMC MIDTOWN CAMPUS.

I was waiting for a call. I started calling the hospital around 9:30 pm. Finally I got a call from a doctor telling me that my husband was very critical and asking me how soon I could get there . I got there and was asked to wait.. They were working on him. I began to pray and walk back and forth near the front door. I did not go to the waiting area because they said COVID was at an all-time high. I was growing tired. I walked over to the security booth and asked if I could go back. I just wanted to put oil on him and pray for him. "Please", pleaded. One of the security guys took me to see Russ. I was not looking forward to this; they only let one person in. I saw my husband laying there and I touched him. He was so cold. He was on the ventilator. The doctor said, "He is a sick man." Russ had already coded twice at that point. I went numb. I felt he had already slipped away. I asked could my sons and brother-in-law come see him. I did not make it home before I was called and told he needed more blood and dialysis. They asked me for an advance directive. Russ and I had a conversation just the week before. "If something happens, what do you want me to do?" I asked him.. He said, "Do all you can do but I do not want you visiting me on machines every day."

I went to visit him the next day and the doctor kept saying he was a very sick man and it looked like every tube and device was attached to him. It saddened me to see my husband of 31 years in that state. I went home and began to have a conversation with God. Prayer Is just a conversation with God. I prayed, "God, please do what you need to do."

I shared all this to say please love on your loved ones. Russ did not get a chance to say goodbye to us but we know he is watching over us as our Guardian ANGEL.

These days, I often recall when I first met Russ. I was sitting on my front porch. He was walking towards the park.

I asked him if I could see his class ring and he let me see it and I tried it on. Me being the loveable person I am, I spoke and that was history. He had a loveable voice. I was wowed that day. We began to talk on the phone every day and sometimes I would fall asleep listening to him on the phone. I confided in my Aunt Neicy. He was older, so I felt a type of way. My family went on a family trip. I stayed with my aunt so I could get to see and spend time with him. Our first date was at Burke's Restaurant downtown Baltimore. We enjoyed a nice meal and we also walked along the harbor. We started a tradition of going to the harbor every Sunday. , and we walked sometimes or we took the water taxi to the other side just to get around. We used public transportation a lot until my dad gave me my first vehicle, a Ford Tempo. Russ didn't have a license but it was ok it worked out. I drove on all our dates. He always had something nice to say and was a gentleman. Few words and quiet. We were high school sweethearts. He went to my ring dance and my Senior Prom. He worked a lot, so we spent a lot of time on the phone. He was a hard worker. He loved to make his money and buy me presents and flowers. I still love flowers to this day.

Women, we can experience the loss of a loved one and still live life. We need to give ourselves permission to live again. Remembering that we all have a beginning and end time. I know my Love would want me to continue living life to the fullest. I continue to put God first in my life. I would like to start a women's group with other widows so we can share our stories. Helping each other out would make us powerful in these times.

So, stay tuned for a women's group coming out of my healing journey. From pain to purpose that's what happens after a loss. Life goes on, the memory will always be with us to help us to make it. I have started a text ministry. I wanted people to know during these trying times that they are not alone, and God is with us. He loves us so much. I remind them every day to trust him and totally rely on him. When I get doubtful, I just look back on all the good times God made a way when there seemed to be no way.

As I am writing this chapter, grief continues to hit at an all-time high. My husband's best friend and best man at our wedding passed away while I was away on a mini vacation at our second home, Atlantic City. As I think of Russ and his best friend and my sons. I consider this fact… grief affects boys and men differently than women. Boys or men hold it in and try hard to play tough when they need to talk to someone and let it out. It is hard to get your grown adult children to at least talk to someone about how they are feeling and not hold it in. Men seem to always try to be hard because a lot of them were taught that if you cried or shed a tear you were less than a man. I always taught my sons that they are human, and they have feelings and emotions; so deal with them, so they won't deal with you.

I am doing a lot of things that I want to do because time is not waiting on anyone, it is moving and fast, too. Places you like to see or visit, schedule the time and take time off to enjoy life with family and friends. Be brave and meet new people along the way. I try to meet up with my grown sons at least twice a week. We do Tuesday Trivia at a local bar and grill. It was started by my oldest. He took a sabbatical for about 6 weeks, so I called on other family members to help us. I am going to start walking with my coworker when school starts back in fall. I had to stop exercising. I had an injury from dropping a bowling ball on my foot and it required therapy and not being able to put a lot of pressure on it. With comfortable shoes, I am going to try to make it work and hopefully lose a couple pounds in the process. I believe I can do this weight loss thing so my knees and hip can support this body. Women are born nurturers, so they love to help other people. I know people always call on me to ask for advice or I just listen today. I think I will continue to seek God's guidance for my future.

I know God wants me to live fully and take good care of myself. I love the healing suggestion to schedule a date with yourself. Take care of yourself. Make an appointment for a massage, a pedicure, and get your hair done. All ways to do self-care.

Being a caregiver like I was for so many years, you lose yourself.
So, I am on the mends getting my mind right and being fed spiritually. Getting used to my new normal of making decisions that will affect me for the rest of my life. I'm realizing I can still do what I have not done ~ it's not too late."

As I continue to write, I am being attacked on every side with distractions. Got another call, another death. My friends try to keep me grounded on moving forward. They call and ask if I registered for that class time. Time has gotten away and I missed the deadline for registration. I will start next semester.

My husband has been gone for over a year now. The word death and grief hits in a whole different way. I have had so many this past year. I continue to turn to God. He is the one that can keep me in this storm. I feel good one day. The next day I feel the grief trying to overtake me. But I rise above it. I move on. The theme of my church this year was MANIFESTING OUR VISION EVERYDAY.

As I am completing this chapter, I ride into work thinking about all the people who have lost a loved one. Grief is hard and it's a process to remember yourself and take care of you. You only get one chance to live in this world. Live it to the fullest. Have no regrets. My new motto, like Nike says, JUST DO IT! PLEASE REMEMBER PUT GOD FIRST IN EVERYTHING HE WILL WORK IT OUT. WE GO THROUGH SOME SAD TIMES BUT THE STORM WILL PASS AND WE WILL PUSH THROUGH. I'M LIVING AGAIN AFTER THE LOST.

Tammy T. Sapp

T ammy Terrelle Sapp, Tammy to her friends and family is a mom, widow, warrior, and published author. Born and raised in Baltimore, Maryland. Tammy graduated from Western High School. She is credentialled in Early Childhood Development and has been working in the education field for over 28 years. Tammy is an administrative assistant at the Sheppard Pratt School where she continues to wear many hats. She is currently a member of the Anointed House of Prayer where she serves in the outreach ministry The Help Outreach Center, THOR. She also loves to pray for people. Tammy is a big witness that prayer works. She has been a part of the

5am Prayer Line for 29 years. During the Pandemic, she started a text ministry where she personally texts daily encouraging words. Tammy started the text ministry to serve, "I didn't want anyone to feel alone when the world was shut down." She didn't miss a beat, understanding some only get this one word of encouragement, so they look forward to a friendly message.

https://linktr.ee/tammy1206
Tammy.sapp@yahoo.com
Tammysapp50@gmail.com

Finding the Stories that Heal You
Kelly Schwartz Keville

W hat did you love to do as a child?"

Bikes, playing with dolls, running, playing outside, imaging things were not *just* what they seemed ~ my responses leap to the front of my brain with vivid moving pictures and emotions I can touch.

The air whipping my hair back, my palms sweating as I hold tight to the rubber covers on the handlebars, foil streamers seemingly burst from the ends of each side. I'm pumping my legs fast downhill; the spinning pedals can't keep up with my feet, so I lean my body back just a bit on the banana seat and throw my legs out wide. Flying past my friends on their bikes trying desperately to keep up with me, laughter escapes and I shout, "Woo Hoo!"

The group leader asks the question, again, "What did you love to do as a child?"

I scan the faces on my Zoom screen each woman in her little box remembering. It's almost instantaneous, the screens seem to brighten, the colors deepen, energy begins to bounce square to square, face to face, smile to smile. Some of us are giggling, all of us are sitting up in our seats as we collectively recall moments in time when we existed free and unencumbered.

"Let's go around. Kel, you're first," our mentor is looking at me. "What did you love to do as a child?"

"I absolutely loved riding bikes. In fact, I still absolutely love riding bikes. When we take our annual family beach trip, one of the first things my sister and I do is head to Mike's Bikes in Fenwick, Delaware to rent beach cruisers for the week. And running, I loved to run."

She asks if I'm a runner now. "Oh, no! I don't mean running for exercise or sport. I mean full-on running just for fun across a big open field, arms flailing, laughing with the pure enjoyment of allowing your body to move freely, unchecked by anyone else's gaze."

As we move around the Hollywood Squares of our Zoom call, each woman takes us back with her for just a moment to share what she loved to do as a child, and we notice some common threads between all our stories. All our stories included opportunities to play, connect with nature, and use our imaginations free of judgement. And with each woman's willingness to tell her story, we each received some healing.

Sharing our short stories of even just one childhood joy brought an easy comfort to the storyteller and her audience. Further connecting us to one another, encouraging us to believe and understand we are not alone. It is a beautiful example of how our stories become the bricks that build our relationships and our communities.

This nurturing, healing magic is always available to us, for us. And I am blessed because I have always innately understood the gift of stories ~ the telling, the writing, the listening, the reading.

Sitting at the counter in our brown apartment kitchen on 85th Avenue, quietly eating my peanut butter and jelly on Wonder Bread, I listen. I watch. My mother with her brown hair curled, brushed, and sprayed stiff leans across the Formica tabletop to hold my Aunt Elise's hand. Aunt Elise is bent forward, her shoulders rolled into her body, guarding her chest which is heaving with deep shallow breaths.

Even at 3 years old, I understand this posture. She's trying to hide her tears and sadness. My aunt whispers about Jimmy and how long he's been gone and a faraway place, the name begins with the letter V. My mother whispers back, "He'll be home soon. I'm here. I will help with the children." Concern grows in me as I watch these two women take turns talking intently with one another and then relief washes over all of us when my mother pushes the chair back the metal legs squeaking across the vinyl floor only to pull it back closer to my auntie. She leans in again, wraps her arms around my aunt who leans in closer, too, accepting my mother's embrace. I marvel at the contrast of their bouffant hair, one strawberry blond and one deep brown. I marvel at the comfort, the healing between them. I'm learning about conversations between women and the ways of storytelling.

The following year, I began to read. I couldn't wait to read books. By all accounts, I was an early reader. Devouring the entire weighty hardcover, Dick and Jane chapter book as my first reading accomplishment. Squeezing onto the cushion between my mother and the arm of the couch close to the lamp I read the entire book aloud, all six chapters.

My mother appreciated my love of reading. She, herself, was always in the middle of reading a book. Early in the morning or late at night, I might find her sitting by the warm lamp light reading but the rest of the day while she worked and mothered, the book would sit nearby on the edge of the kitchen countertop or maybe on one of the oak end tables in the living room or perhaps, I would find "her book" on the bedside nightstand or on occasion, soaking wet lying open over the edge of the bath tub (she loved reading in the tub but the warm water made her ever so sleepy after a long day). She often bragged that as a child she would walk around trying to complete her chores while continuing to read "her book" and her mother would scold her, "Carolyn! Get your nose out of that book." Clearly, Nana Grace didn't have the same affinity for reading books, but she was, in fact, one of my favorite storytellers.

While my mother fancied romantic books of happiness and love, Nana Grace would share the dark hard truth of her often-painful childhood, cradled in the blessings of what was to come. As soon as we were old enough, she began sharing her stories of abandonment, starvation, and violence at the hands of a rageful alcoholic father, coupled with stories of wise good witches living in the woods that healed wounds with suave and anonymous good Samaritans leaving baskets heavy with food and warm clothes on their rickety wooden porch, games Nana Grace played in the woods with her three brothers and two sisters, and a gentle, kind mother appropriately named Effie Joy.

Stories come to us through family, friends, and strangers. Stories come to us through spoken words passed down through the generations. And they come to us through written words. The written stories have an extra superpower, they can reach far and wide, out of ear shot, forever immortalizing the "characters" and their experience, strength, and hope.

The intimate act of literally writing our stories first takes the storyteller deeper, deeper in her connection to self and then, once she bravely walks thru her story on her own, the desire to share what she has unearthed will continue to pull her into deeper connection with others. She knows the healing must be shared.

I believe storytelling IS the language of women. We are the keepers of the story. In our conversations, we share our stories like housewarming gifts, welcoming one another into our homes, into ourselves. I give you one, you give one back and the exchange becomes the foundation of friendship and love between us. Of course, the stories must hold authentic truth as we understand it and with this generosity, healing is offered to us all.

Writing in community has proven to be the most amazing combination of sharing our powerful stories through both the spoken and written word. We gather, we write independently, we read our words aloud, we write more, we read more, we catalog our "work" in file folders or digital folders or maybe we print our stories and place the sheets of paper into a special box or drawer. We line our desks and bookshelves with stacks of full journals and notebooks. And sometimes we hear the call to take things one step further and we publish our work. The words have power in all their forms intentional or unintentional, conversations or publications. I choose to be intentional with my words and my stories. Here's an invitation for you to join me.

Take a simple, well-crafted question or word or an image, carve out 10 minutes, take pencil and paper to a comfortable writing space, and write. Write with abandon. Give yourself permission to dive into your stories without judgement. Write. Don't think, just write. Don't worry about correct punctuation or grammar, make a quick note if you feel compelled to fact check. Keep the pencil moving on the paper.

What? The words are not flowing? Stop thinking, just write. Remember, the physical act of using a pencil and paper allows you to engage your creativity more readily because it helps quiet the other thinking part of your brain, much like when you get your best ideas in the shower or driving your car on a familiar route. You can write the question or the prompt over and over again. You could write, "I don't want to write. I can't think of anything to write." You can simply doodle or draw spirals. Keep your hand moving and you'll see, if you allow yourself to write with abandon, something will come. Some knowing will find its way to the paper. You may have to look through some extra words or weird punctuation or incorrect spelling but I guarantee you will see something.

I have the perfect example for you. Recently, I was caught "in my head", ruminating on reoccurring struggles in my life, namely my dissatisfaction with my body and my bank account. With this discontent whirling around in my head causing me such angst, I decided to do what I do when I'm dealing with unpleasant overwhelm and chaos. I decided to start writing. Get ready, here is a vulnerable excerpt of a first draft which "downloaded" thru my pencil onto the paper:

It's 2:00pm on a typical Tuesday. I've been working from my glass kitchen table all morning: writing my chapter for my third multi-author book, attending assorted virtual Zoom call meetings, posting on social media, but mostly, I've been thinking thoughts.

As I snap back to reality, I open my honey brown leather day planner with TWO THOUSAND TWENTY THREE professionally embossed in gold on the cover.

My calendar reminds me I need to go to the Post Office to return a dress my daughter ordered weeks ago. I promised I would take care of it for her while she studies abroad. Per usual, it has been sitting in my car for weeks. "What kind of lame mother are you, Kelly? Do you EVER do what you say you are going to do? Why does everything take so long with you? You are pathetic."

Motivated by feelings of unworthiness, I hurriedly push my chair back, step into my Florida flip flops, and grab my purse and keys. Believing somehow, I may prove my worth with this one small gesture.

Outside the warm sun is delightful on my face and my chest. I breathe deeply for the first time all day it seems. "You've got to get outside more," I berate myself. "All you do is sit on your butt! No wonder you are getting so fat." The black 2008 Honda Accord stares at me with its broken headlight and fading scratched paint. Opening the driver's side door, the cracked leather seats scream, "You are a broke bitch!"

"UGH, I hate this car," I say under my breath.

"No, Kelly. Gratitude! You love this car even with its imperfections, it has saved you years of car payments and despite the oil burning engine, it miraculously continues to get you where you need to go. Be grateful for your blessings. You will never be blessed with more, if you don't appreciate what you already have," I admonish myself.

As I drive out of my development, I'm suddenly starving. I know I should save money and I want to eat a cheeseburger, right now. I know I should support my body with healthier food. And I want to indulge myself with fast food. Right now! Emotional eating? Perhaps. What feels like a primal need to eat, gets loud and rowdy, and discourages me from waiting until I get back home to eat the piles of less expensive, healthy food stacked in my refrigerator and in my pantry. My "hunger" demands a sandwich at the fast food joint I will be passing in just 3 minutes with an oh-so-convenient drive-thru entrance right off the road.

My sister, Jenny, calls me as I pull up to the giant sign squawking at me, "Can I take your order?" Quickly, before I place my order, I place my thrifty, superhuman frugal sister on hold, "Why yes you can. I'll have the number 7, large fries, and large Coke, light ice." The young woman shouts back thru the scratchy sound system, "Is that all?" I think, "Is that all? What do I look like a 250lb truck driver?" I answer myself, "Yes, apparently, you do." Then, I politely respond to the woman taking my order, "Yes, thank you." I click off mute and tell my sister, I'll give her a call back when I get home.

But the dialogue in my head starts, "Ewww, what are you doing? All that fast food is terrible for you. Remember, you can clean the dirt and oil and road grime from your hubcaps with that large Coke, think about what it is doing to your teeth. Your teeth are looking kinda yellow, and stained. You are getting so fat. You are almost bigger than you were the day you delivered your first baby. What a pathetic waste. You suck! You are ugly and fat and stupid and weak, and you deserve all the shitty shit you get. You look like a disgusting old witch. You are so gross."

My writing doesn't always deliver such clear previously unobserved self-knowledge, but this piece made me cry as I read it aloud to myself. Until I saw it written on the page and then heard myself read the words, I didn't realize how cruelly I had been speaking to myself. If you asked me, I would tell you what I know intellectually, negative self-talk is detrimental, and I don't do it. I would tell you how I reassure myself and often say aloud, "You're OK, Kelly. Everything is going to be fine." But this internal voice was sneaky and insidious, cloaked in my unconscious and until I allowed myself to write with abandon, it remained unconscious. The excavation was unexpected and what surfaced was wisdom. I unearthed something I couldn't see before and this knowledge, this data is helping me to be more intentional in my storytelling. Writing the stories that hurt us, helps us to write the stories that heal us.

One more suggestion to support you through this process... be generous in spirit with yourself, find the little child in you. I'm sure she's there. Keep looking... where is she? What does she look like? What is her hair color, her eye color? What does she love to do?

Now, write with abandon. Come on, you've got this.

I'll share first...

She's beautiful, I marvel at her perfection, smooth tan skin, soft round cheeks, light sea blue green eyes, her warm brown hair shimmering with golden strands brushes her shoulders as she dances by. She sneaks around behind me and tickles my back with her little girl hands. She giggles and covers her mouth but her smiling eyes shine and give her away. I turn quickly to catch her reaching out to hold her but she wiggles free and spins and twirls and finally leaps back towards me grabbing my hand and pulling me along to follow her deeply into the meadow where she throws herself gently down into the pasture of wild flowers and golden green grass. The dandelion wishes fly up and over us like tiny fairies as I lay down on my back next to her. I look over our green eyes seeing one another and then we look back up to the blue open sky, and we laugh.

I encourage you to find a writing mentor and a writer's community, you are always welcome to join me. All my contact information is readily available in my bio. But whatever you do, get intentional with the stories you tell yourself and others. Gather your tribe and acknowledge the wealth of wisdom resting in you. Step into your power and potential. Find the stories that heal you.

Kelly Schwartz Keville

K elly Schwartz Keville is a published author and creative, social entrepreneur with a passion for empowering women and raising the quality of life for them and their children. Kelly graduated from Loyola University with a degree in writing/sociology. She has spent much of her professional career working in the field of child development and early education. In 2020, Kelly started her own business as a women's empowerment coach and a writing mentor.

Kelly's new podcast titled What's Your Story, Morning Glory allows her to do what she loves most; connecting, creating, and collaborating with other women.

Through her writing and her life coaching business, Kelly guides her clients to live an intentional life; stepping into their power and potential ~ every day. She believes embodying a true, deep self-love is the foundation for all the best things in life.

Kelly lives in the Baltimore/Washington Metropolitan area with her four beautiful children ~ John Michael, Savannah, Ben, and Scott.

kellyschwartzkeville@gmail.com
https://linktr.ee/kellyschwartzkeville
https://www.instagram.com/kellyschwartzkeville
https://www.facebook.com/kelly.a.keville

Inner Connected
Elizabeth Page Shepley

Edge to the Stars

(a monologue for teenage schemes and dreams)

I choose not to be reckless. I don't smoke or drink or do drugs. I am responsible. I get things done. I keep my friends in line. They tell me their secrets. My parents trust me or they're just too consumed by their own demons to worry about mine. I've got it together.

Yet, sometimes when the sun goes down, cloaked in the darkness of midnight, reckless impulses stir within me, and deviance surges to the surface. If I don't move on it, do something, do anything to take the edge off, then I might do everything and die.

I cover every piece of my body in solid black clothing and pull a black ski cap over my ears. Only my white face shows. I meet Shadow for a midnight rendezvous under the stars. The blacktop road a hundred feet from my front doorsteps is our dance floor, and our moves look exactly like a resting corpse. Carpenter Road gets quiet at midnight, but it isn't unreasonable that a few cars will speed by on their way to the highway, especially since that 24-hour Walmart Supercenter was opened.

As I lay there not moving a muscle, my body melts into the manmade slab between me and Mother Earth. The stars are piercing in this deep darkness. At first, they sting my eyes like tiny needles, then they soften. I soften. The vastness of the sky and multitudes of stars transform from something big and scary and unknown into something of magic and boundless possibility. It soothes me.

I remember when I first heard the term "straight edge." This guy, straight out of New York and branded with a single tattoo on his bare shoulder, looked so badass, and I watched as he was offered a beer while he waited for a late car repair on his way to a rock festival somewhere in Florida. He flashed his tattoo and said, "I'm good." My observation and curiosity weren't to be silenced, and I walked my uncool teenage self over and asked about the tattoo: little s, big X, little e as one word in black ink and a sharp font. He surprised me by offering a generous smile. "The s and e are short for 'straight edge,' and the X means no drugs, tobacco or alcohol." My eyes widened as he laughed and walked away. I went back to my work in the office.

Of course, I knew Christians who didn't smoke or drink or anything, or at least ones who claimed that, but the people out in the world making the most noise were touting drugs and sex. It was liberating to consider hardcore punk rockers who push past the edges through their creative expression and turn their backs on the social hype that getting wasted was to live. I decided "straight edge" was an identifier I could adopt. I'd stop visiting the vodka bottle when no one was looking and I couldn't deal with my family for one more sober minute. I decided I don't have to follow in their footsteps. I would be straight edge in my own expression, without the punk. I'd take my frustrations to the page. I'd bring them to the stage. I'd look in the mirror and tell her that I see her and we can get through the discomfort without numbing it. I'd feel it all. However hard. I'd prove my commitment one hard choice after hard choice. Straight edge.

One star becomes brighter, maybe moving closer to me; undeniably commanding my attention. I lock in. Focused on this tiny speck of Light above me, I can't tell where I end and the road or sky begin. I dissolve into the black sky becoming one with the stars. At once I am Stardust and see lines connecting the matter that is me to all that is. The edge dissolves. It does not matter where I end and the rest begins or ends. What is clear is that I matter.

The roar of a diesel engine coming around the curve about a half a mile South pulls me back to the hard road I lay on, and my mind's eye traces the edges of my body, and I wiggle my fingers and toes. I pull a flashlight from my pocket and switch on the Light.

Hello World. I'm still here.

Growing into Quiet

Some days I feel like Dr. Seuss's Grinch, "Oh, the Noise! Noise! Noise!

Noise!" The small sounds in the house become amplified. Denali's collar clanks against her stainless-steel water bowl. Linus's nervous throat clearing growls through the hallway. Willow jumps on the table and commands treats and pets. Kids scream next door. Music and yelling bellow from the television screen where Pete plays some kind of video game, and I find myself wishing for a mute button for the normal activities of daily living.

When Staples had an "easy button," I often wished they'd supply something similar that would drop a soundproof box around me, but often I'd find myself on edge with more sounds swirling in my head than in my actual physical space. My mental script is pretty standard from what other expressive humans share about living in this busy, high-pressured culture. "I should've done this. I can't do that. There's not enough for those. Why isn't there more time? Why can't I take a nap? What is the point? You'll never make it..." It all gets so loud. For the longest time, most of my life, I didn't know any other way.

All my childhood and young adult years were spent striving for excellence and becoming the best fill-in-the-blank whatever I stepped into. Encouragement and criticism all made the same noise. I couldn't tell the difference between a compliment, a joke, an instruction, or a critique. For a long time, I didn't even know what quiet was because there was so much disruption outside, inside. It can make a person feel sideways. Even my "good girl" response to a commanding shush was as piercing as the school fire alarm.

Little by little, I became aware of the script, and my being started to shift. My being settled and let go of busyness and found a quiet spot at the Ocean. That expanded to a quiet minute in the car. A quiet moment by the mailbox. In the shower. With my morning cup of coffee. Cultivating mindful spaces throughout my day.

I have learned to tune inward to find quiet. The sounds from the physical atmosphere fade, and all the noise of social expectations melt away. A spaciousness opens inside, and I resist the urge to fill the silence with anything superficial. It is not uncomfortable here. I cozy into it. I feel the earth beneath me, and I trust our connection. I feel the cosmos above me, and I trust our connection too. It is the most connected I feel out of all the places and scenes. I guess it's the opposite of the saying about feeling alone in a crowded room. I feel connected in solitude. Beneath all the noise out there, I have this calm knowing in here. One that is rooted in love.

Learning to drop in when I need to resource requests for consistent practice. Sometimes we forget what helps us most. Sometimes the noise and sensory overwhelm drown out our sensibility. Just when I feel like I've found a good process and rhythm, I get a new opportunity to grow, to expand the toolbox, to develop more skill, to apply things in a different way to an entirely new situation. I know there is no possible way to reach mastery which is both humbling and discouraging.

I sometimes hear the echoes of words spoken a decade earlier, and it feels as if I'm hearing them for the first time ever because it is finally quiet enough that their impact has caught up with me. I can work with this awareness. Aware of the impact I can begin to accept how the script serves or hinders my being, and I can let go of things that no longer support me. I can grant airtime to the loving messages that stick with me, even if I couldn't hear them in real time, and I can gift myself quiet moments coasting in neutral allowing any sound to just flow through my windows. I can consider those things that stick in my ears and in my deeper hearing sense, approaching them with curiosity, releasing any judgment, and I can emerge from my quiet moments transformed and fortified. Speaking, doing, writing, being my own message of love.

Lessons *by Elizabeth Shepley*

The Ocean roars beyond this bend,
calling to wash away the weight of my story.
With every step, the load feels lighter,
and my feet carry me closer,
eyes locked in the stone cold depth of these waters.
The knots in my gut release, my jaw loosens,
and the sudden wonder full smile across my face
would embarrass a clown.

Bands of icy sea foam line the water's edge.
Crunchy, playful bubbles offer to cleanse
the mucky energy I brought in.
A chunk breaks free and circles my feet
reminding me that I too am free.
That I too can break through this cold bond
and live my joy.
That I can be with lightness
and exist with delicacy without breaking.

99

The Ocean, she shows me that I am not alone or misunderstood,
so I dance and sing Her a song of gratitude.

Home Making from the Inside Out

Homemade love bubbles through me. I make it. I mix it using recipes left to me and ingredients harvested from me and materials sourced by me. I'm crafting my own way here and just hope that as people come through they will take a slice and remember some sweet morsel of themselves. The goods I'm serving do not contain any secret ingredients or special sauce. This is just a messy buffet of homemade love.

Every dish made was once an idea. A beginner's mind has a dash of innocence, and each recipe is made from scratch through the experiments of the maker–a homemade, homegrown treat delivered with love. No cutting corners to get there. The best batches are served fresh and shared in love.

Most recipes happen organically. Noticing what is available. Pulling in the staples and adding this and that for a little flavor. Trusting that it'll come together one ingredient at a time. Allowing the process and being in it, being with it. The product is a side effect. The ingredients and tender construction, infused with gratitude, dish up a feast for the senses.

Some recipes don't work out, and sometimes the whole pot may get scorched and tossed. Some folks just don't like what's on the table. Sometimes the cookies are just too hard, and sometimes the cake sinks.

Listing it all out like that there's not much reason to keep on cookin'. I might choose to hang my apron, toss my spoon and dim the kitchen lights–taken down by the expense of it all. I choose what to serve here. I get to restock and keep cooking because life is going to keep coming at me. The world will keep on, and I can hide in the dark, cold pantry, but every time I start to step away something whispers to me, pulling me back, "A lil' bit of something sweet rises from every act of creation." I keep on experimenting, sourcing strength, resilience and curiosity.

Scrumptious crumbs of homemade love are baked right into these walls, and even when the lights are out, the cookies are on the table and hot soup is only a few minutes away. In Braving the Wilderness, Brene Brown talks about learning what it means to have a "Strong back; soft front; wild heart." After nearly four decades of growing up, I feel myself growing down, and what has been homemade is taking root. I'm grounding into my wilderness, and it feels paradoxical for this transformation to come through the kitchen: the seat for feminine domestication. Yes, and I'm here for it. At my post. Ready or not. Brave and still afraid. Cultivating enough homemade love to share with my loved ones and neighbors and strangers.

I unfold a worn page tucked in my apron pocket: an open invitation to celebrate. I pack a wealth of recipes, some original and some found, all instilled with my own experience. I reflect on what I've cooked up in this life so far and all the messes I've made and how they've served me. I set the table and add a touch of festivity and breathe into my invitation celebrating all that I see.

Welcome to My Work…and Yours

(a dialog calling you in across time and space from a cozy cabin like kitchen area)

Just come on in, the door's open! I'm in the kitchen. I just took some homemade chocolate chip cookies out of the oven. Can I get you a cup of tea? Coffee? Help yourself to the tea box there on the counter. I'll pour the water.

I'm just giddy that you've stopped back in while I'm here, and we get to connect. Your note said that you have some questions about the poem, My Work, that I posted on the blog. Let's get cozy, and you can tell me more about that, and I will share what's true for me.

Oh thank you! I love the owls too! Making them brings me so much joy. They started as a little project to use to decorate this place and gift our visitors a sense of my scrappy, resourceful style, and I just love the process so much. I can't stop making owls from whatever scraps and bits blow my way. *wink*

"Alright Alright Alright" –that's my best Matthew McConaughey impression for ya. Where would you like to begin?

Read the poem aloud? oof yes I can. Here it goes:

My Work

My work is about me.

Pausing in the discomfort,

102

Holding the tension,
I stretch in the freedom
to breathe.
Peeling away layers of muck,
Choosing my hard, my truth,
I feel into the purpose
to love.

Redefining relationship with the world,
Challenging everything I was taught,
I lean into the clarity
to know.

Without me, there is no meaning.

Jinkees! It makes me quiver every time, and my heart speeds up like a bunny in panic mode trying to find a way out.

I suspect it happens because this idea that "my work is about me" goes against everything I've ever been taught about being a good woman and mother. You're supposed to be selfless and make personal sacrifices to keep the peace and take care of everybody else. To show love is to be giving even if it is the last bit you've got to give.

That sounds so unreasonable when I say it out loud. I'd never define a "good woman" according to these criteria if I were speaking about any single other woman I know. Thank you for this invitation.

Yes, I've learned that building meaningful relationships with the wider world means having a relationship with myself first, and when I asked this human in the mirror what she values in a relationship, she actually has a lot to say about it. Can you imagine that? *wink* And the simplest most basic element is trust and honesty. As I explored this more through my own creative practice of journaling and collage and mark making, I realized that at the root of my "trust issues" was a belief that to show up for others I had to abandon this woman —abandon what was true and good and right for me.

That is the point where things got interesting. When I pulled that baggage out of the closet into the Light I realized it was packed around a myth, and unpacking that and letting go of the pieces that were not serving me gave me space to begin again with an awareness and acceptance that when I abandon myself to "keep the peace" with others then I choose suffering for myself. When I'm in the midst of suffering, it is almost impossible to feel that my life is meaningful, and despair is only a footstep away. I love these words by Elizabeth Gilbert, "And yet, when we do suffer and we come through it, oftentimes we can't help but see where there was something in that suffering that had to happen…I would say that sometimes suffering is actually part of the wonder, the tool of suffering and what it can turn you into."

This is the foundational work. That's what is here beneath my feet at the foundation of this space I'm building and that's what our offer of genuine hospitality really means—you have an invitation here to explore what's true for you at the core beneath all the baggage, all the layers.

This is my work. That's where I found my footing and that's when I saw that the woman in the mirror deserves peace. We all deserve peace. I've been here learning how to make it for myself, so I've got some ideas to share when it feels right, but mostly, I'll be here to speak kindly to you when you feel you haven't got the strength to do it for yourself, and I'll be with you while you learn to walk with your own expression. And I'll serve fresh cookies and a warm hug in a mug every day.

Elizabeth Page Shepley

E lizabeth Page Shepley is an author, creative living coach and contemporary shaman supporting the helpers, the healers, writers and artists to restore a deeper relationship with their core being so that they may show up more fully in their life and work. Offering a loving, compassionate space, Elizabeth invites clients to get honest about what's holding them back, so that they can move into a more committed relationship with their Higher Self. She offers private and small group coaching, meetups and expressive arts workshops to integrate the creative process into the rhythm of daily life. If it feels right, stop by any of these online spaces to receive a helping of genuine hospitality and soulful creative connection.

Website: https://owl-create.com/
Email: elizabeth@owl-create.com

Schedule a complimentary curiosity call:
https://calendly.com/owlcreate
https://vimeo.com/owlcr8
https://www.facebook.com/owl.create.coaching
https://www.instagram.com/owl.create.coaching/

My Tree of Happy
Shannon Sheridan

S itting in my bed, I wrote a letter to God. I was in a very dark place, and I knew I had to get out. This was a powerful move for me because I was not one to believe in religion or God. I could never say that I was "atheist", so I was that girl that claimed she was "agnostic". I knew there was something greater, I just was never taught correctly. The tears streamed down my puffy red face. I asked God to please help me get out of this mess I created. The pain was too much to bear and my soul was hurting. I could not continue the torture I was putting myself through. I had become so distant from who I was, and I knew I had to find myself again. Everything I was doing was everything I would have never imagined myself doing growing up. The people around me were not people I would recommend anyone be around, and my gut was telling me to get out. I knew I had to make some huge life changes and I knew the strength was there, I just needed a little help. So, I wrote my letter and put it under my mattress and fell asleep. Thank you, God, for answering my letter. Just being able to sit and type this chapter and admit I am an addict in recovery, I thank you for that blessing.

The year 2020 was full of transformation for me. My addiction was not out in the open at all and I hid it with alcohol and depression. This nasty habit consisted of all things bad up my nose, and I hid it so well. I would stay up all hours of the night and it got so bad that I was starting to hallucinate. That is when I got to my point of surrender. I was living two lives for way too long and I had had enough. I was in the middle of my thirties, a single mom of two boys, and I had given up on men. I had lost myself years back after I broke up with my youngest son's father. I was told so many times by him that I would never find someone who loves me because I had two kids from two different fathers already, and who would want to be with someone like that. My trust in men was zero. I was at a very low point in my life and had very low self-esteem. I was so unhealthy, and my skin was an absolute mess. Deep down inside, I knew my worth and so my addiction and my wrongful actions were killing me on the inside. Knowing my worth and having those baby boys to take care of is where my strength came from. I knew it was now my time to become the best version of myself. This was my chance, and I started to climb that mountain in 2020 secretly, and all on my own.

My first step was cutting out all the people in my life that were not serving my highest good. I basically had zero friends that I trusted at that time. Looking back, it was easy to let them go as they were all doing horrible things and getting caught up in them, so I had no choice but to leave and not get caught up in their messes. I had my own mess to get out of, my own addiction to fight. Once they were gone, magically my life started to piece back together a little at a time. It was lonely and hard, but I knew the whole time that I was making the correct decision. I also had to learn that they were not the only ones to blame, and that I had some hard work to handle within myself. I started to realize that my past is my past and if I am moving forward, things will come together as they should. I then started to focus on myself and my boys and just being the best me I possibly could. I cleared a lot of negatives out of my life, and I was left with what I needed to correct inside myself.

It was now the middle of 2020, and I had become sober from drugs all on my own. I did it! I was so proud of myself for clearing those demons out of my life. In June 2020, my boyfriend at the time took me on a trip that I will never forget. This trip up to the Sierra Mountains, CA was one that changed my life forever. It was the highest peak of my healing journey and a trip I will never forget. This trip brought me back to life almost as if I was a dormant tree waiting to be watered. On this random weekend getaway, my roots grew deep into the Earth, and I connected back with the trees and nature. I was sober from all things illegal, and it felt so good, but there was still a part of me that was struggling. I did not feel deserving. I was still hiding a huge secret from everyone I love, and that was my addiction. Even though I was sober, the guilt and shame were still very raw. I went up those mountains with a lot of built-up fear and emotions, and I came down with them pouring out of me.

It was such a gorgeous day as we loaded up the car to go on this trip up to the Sierra Mountains. With a 6-hour drive ahead of us, reggae music playing, and the sun shining, we headed up the 101 North freeway to our destination high in altitude. The weather was perfect in California, as usual. The outside world seemed so chaotic because of what they called a pandemic, and it was always a challenge for me going out in the midst of all that mess. I knew something was not right in the world. I was learning new things and I was unlearning a lot of things I had thought were real. I felt I had to stand up for what I believed in. I was excited for the trip but also very nervous and my anxiety was high, but I was glad to get out of my normal routine. My normal routine consisted of working and masking my problems with alcohol and finding anything to make me happy to not think about my past. I was in a better place than I had been one year ago, but I still had so much pain inside to clear out and face. This trip was needed, and little did I know, this trip would change my life in so many ways.

Traveling during this time was frustrating as bathrooms were limited for some strange reason, always out of order, and signs were plastered everywhere making you wear a mask to enter any store. My fight for freedom and basic human rights was exhausting and caused a lot of anxiety for me being out in public. Fear was everywhere and I was determined to not live in fear. This trip really pulled a lot of that out of me and showed me my fears straight on. I now realize looking back that those fears of mine were safety, support, and trust. It was hard for me to trust anyone after all I went through in 2019 and all the wisdom I had gathered about the world we all live in. It was especially hard for me to trust men. It was even harder for me to trust myself.

We drove up the 101 freeway, excited to get to our destination. As we headed up in elevation, the trees started to change. There was a period of dry, nothing, open land, and then slowly and suddenly an abundance of gorgeous trees and rocks came into view. The sky was so blue, and the clouds were so beautiful and fluffy in the sky. One of my favorite things to do is to look at the sky and search for images or shapes. Angel wings are always there, protecting us, and I love looking up and seeing that reminder. I also love looking up and seeing hawks flying in the air or sitting on telephone poles. They are my reminders of protection. The wildlife and nature really gave me something to care for and I was so excited to see it all. This was where I started to find my feelings of safety, support, and trust in life, through Mother Earth and everything created from God.

With my head back on the reclined chair, feet up, gazing out the window, I came to realize many things on the drive up to the Sierra Mountains. I am not just lucky to be on this amazing trip, but I realized that I am lucky to be alive. These first months of the year 2020 were monumental in my life as I had just recently released a disgusting habit that was starting to affect me mentally. I was a mess on the inside, and I carried so much guilt and shame up those mountains. I did not feel deserving, and I did not feel worthy. I had it all by the looks of it, but on the inside, I was the only one who knew the hurt I had caused to my body and my family. No one knew the extent of my addiction and the shame and guilt was killing me inside. My values and my morals were thrown away about 7 years ago and I was so mad at myself for letting them go. I was on the beginning road of sobriety from all things illegal and it felt good knowing I was on the right path; that path was like climbing a steep mountain one step at a time. I could feel my innocence coming back but the trauma and guilt was also there bubbling up, I could feel it. Emotions were being suppressed but I could feel the pain from my past needing to be released and let go. I kept trying to suppress these emotions, hoping they would go away. When we arrived at the hotel, it was perfect. There was a cute local fishing store right across from it and we got all the info we needed about where to go and what to do. Our quaint little hotel was right off the highway, and it had a bear statue carved in wood out in front. The grumpy but helpful older lady checked us in, and we headed to our room to rest. The hotel was like a log cabin. There were flowers and trees surrounding the walkway and patio and even a few wooden rocking chairs set up on the porch overlooking the highway. I was excited to rest and take it all in.

My dad would take my younger brother and I camping when we were young, and this trip reminded me of those times. He would take pictures of us hugging trees as we walked around our campground. My surroundings felt the same as if I was a little girl. I was so in awe of the trees. They were so high up in the sky and stood with so much power and beauty. The air felt so crisp and cold, and it felt so healing breathing it in. The smell of pine and dirt was so soothing. Just the smell being outdoors was a reminder I am not where I am used to being. It was sensory overload but in a good way. I felt so lucky to be on the trip and I was in complete shock that I was given this chance in life. I was so proud of myself but also so ashamed and this was such an overwhelming feeling that I just could not keep inside. This trip really slapped me in the face with the reality that everything was not fine just because I was sober from illegal drugs up my nose. This trip was a realization that I had more problems to face, and alcohol and depression were the top two.

Driving through the forest was beautiful but I was getting frustrated as everything was just passing me by. I was done with life passing me by. I wanted to stop and soak it in. I wanted to stop and be there in the moment with the trees, but they all just kept passing me by. I was being called to nature and to just sit but we just kept going and going and I was exhausted. My senses were on overload and my body was not used to being so active. My muscles were aching, and I was struggling with being in the wilderness. I did not feel safe and weird random exaggerated scenarios were going through my head. I could tell that my mental state was not back to normal, and I was struggling. I was struggling with the unknown. Thoughts were going through my head about what the future holds, what I deserve, and what I had done. The highs and lows were exhausting not only in the elevation we traveled but also the highs and lows of my mood. I never knew what to expect on this trip as we were in a new place I had never been before and that caused me extreme anxiety. I know now that I was focusing too much on the past and too much on the future when really my soul was fighting to be in the present moment.

There was one exceptional moment on our trip I will never forget. We were driving down the highway, headed back to our hotel, and there was an open area to my right where trees had been cut down. Some of them had red ribbons around them, and some had orange spray paint. It was like they were picked to die. Their branches and stumps just spread out all over the hillside. One side of the highway was full of life with large trees and birds chirping, then the other side was completely somber and empty. This was the tipping point for my emotions, and I just started bawling right then and there uncontrollably. I couldn't hold it in any longer and when asked why I was crying, I had no idea. I was sad for the trees, but I had never felt a feeling like that before. It was so depressing for me driving by these beautiful massive trees that were just cut down. How could someone just cut down a living tree, just stripping it from its roots deep in the Earth. I could feel the pain and the sadness, and it was overwhelming. I had never felt so connected to nature or trees and from that moment on, I know that my tree of happy will never be cut down. My tree of happy was just starting to come back to life and I was on a comeback mission back to myself, and back to being that little innocent girl walking around the campground, hugging trees. I am my own tree of happy and no one can cut that down unless I let them.

Reflecting on this, there were moments of fear and there were moments of anxiety but I somehow managed to thoroughly enjoy the adventure. There were times when I was so at peace, soaking up the air and the amazing views, but there were also times where I did not feel safe, and I could not understand why. We found multiple lakes where we fished. We drove around and saw so many animals. I was not able to find a bear walking around but I saw deer, turkeys, ducks, and eagles. The trees were my favorite part to look up at. They stood so solid and tall, I looked up to them in that way. I was on my way to being tall, powerful, and strong, I could feel it underneath all the trauma I had to release.

The drive home was different. I felt different. I felt stronger. I felt that I left a part of me up there in those mountains that I needed to release. I conquered my anxiety and got through it all. I was so proud of myself and I was so grateful. I did still have some shame left inside my body, and I knew that my work was not over, and I still had a windy path to follow. Having a secret like that and being deceitful to everyone I knew, really took a toll on my pride and my sense of well-being. I let that go as much as I could, and I was determined to move past these insecurities. I told myself, the past is the past and I am only moving forward NOT backwards. This trip was a catapult in my spiritual and healing journey. Those trees and that fresh air refreshed every single cell in my body, and I was now on a downward slope of healing. I felt as if I could accomplish anything and that the worst was behind me. The knowingness of what I had to do was there and I was so excited for my new life ahead. I knew from this trip on, I can accomplish anything!

I am so proud of myself. I think of myself now as a beautiful crystal that is activated by the sun and grounded by the soil of Mother Earth. I was formed and shaped by intense heat and pressure and that is how I became so brilliant. My energy is love and I shine so bright. I realize now that my brightness has always been there, it just needed to be excavated out from the world trying to cover it up. I will never let my sparkle be hidden. I will continue to heal and shine my light for others to follow in my path, up and down any mountain. My tree of happy will continue to flourish and my roots will continue to grow.

Shannon Sheridan

S hannon is now not only sober from everything illegal but has also been sober from alcohol for over one year! She continues to grow and be the best version of herself. Her passion for freedom and getting healthy has become a lifestyle and she continues to spread awareness and confidence through her social media.

Shannon's new passion for nature, animals, and spirituality has led her to open her own little crystal shop. She loves to learn about crystals and she shares that love with others through her online crystal shop. Her next dream is to own a store one day.

Shannon is also a mom of two young boys. They continue to challenge her and give her purpose to thrive and make the world a better place. She also has a career as a medical biller and has been in that industry for 15 years.

@theshannonsheridan
@stonedwithshannon
Email: Shanlynn004@yahoo.com

Express Yourself Publishing
About Express Yourself Publishing & Hollis Citron

C reativity goes beyond a pencil and a paintbrush" - Hollis Citron
Hello everyone, my name is Hollis Citron. I am so happy that
you are in this space reading and benefiting from the wisdom of these
incredible humans!

A little about me. I have been an art educator for 30 years and have
worked with so many people of all different ages, abilities, and
backgrounds. It has been such a gift. It has really brought to light a
passion and constant reminder to me to be an active listener and
observer to then be a guide for others to have permission to explore
possibilities and feel expressive.

Express Yourself Publishing has been created to enhance the power
and awareness of the written word. People are willing to be vulnerable
as they write and share experiences and perspectives, which is such a
gift to both the writer and reader, and it feels so expansive. I believe

that by people sharing their stories, which as we know is an ancient tradition it binds us together and creates stronger connections on both a physical, psychological, and spiritual level. There is such power in the written word.

The mission here is to shine the spotlight for each individual, both authors and readers, to feel expressive and empowered. We each have stories that shape us but do not have to define us. We are works in progress. I truly believe and have seen it over and over again that when a person sees themself as a creator, they feel purposeful and are at their core happier individuals.

Express Yourself publishing is all about creating that safe space for all to have permission to let your guard down and allow you to explore YOU and quiet that inner voice in your head that may not be so supportive at times, do you know that voice?

Please bring this as a mantra into your life so you can get it into your subconscious and don't let anyone else tell you otherwise...

"I Am Creative... I Am Expressive...I Am Worthy"
Hollis Citron is the Founder & CEO of Express Yourself Publishing & I Am Creative. Check out my podcast, Creative Conversations with Hollis Citron that is all about expanding the definition of creativity beyond a pencil and a paintbrush.

Blake
Book Cover Artist

H ello world. My name is Blake. I'm an artist.

I was born in New York in 1996 and grew up with a steady diet of Pollock, Picasso, Basquiat, Mozart, Beethoven, The Doors, Hendrix, The Beatles.

My bedroom was adjacent to my father's art studio - so my early days were spent creating in his studio with music blasting.

As a child my father gave me art books so images were my world and fascination. Colors were my dreamworld. Matisse's Goldfish were my fish.

We moved to Florida when I was young and it was adventurous. I kept up with my vision in art. In a middle school group art show, a person asked my teacher if she could purchase my work. We sold it - my first sale. Soon after, at the age of 10, I had my first solo art show at a coffee house on Davis Islands - and we sold all 12 pieces for $175 per piece.

I went on to college where I studied art and won a scholarship. My days were spent either in the school studio or my apartment studio. These endless nights of working helped hone my skills. Working 24 hours straight was not uncommon. It was fuel for my imagination.

Since then I have been fortunate to have patrons and many collectors who believe in my work. I feel blessed at this age.

My goal is to beautify the world and leave a mark like Vincent, Basquiat, Monet, Bosch, Kahlo, Pollock, deKooning, Bacon and all my mental mentors.

Much luv,
Blake

Instagram @blakecreates
https://linktr.ee/blakecreates
bmunch6@gmail.com

Made in the USA
Middletown, DE
09 October 2023

40298082R00080